the salvage studio

the salvage studio

Sustainable Home Comforts to Organize, Entertain, and Inspire

By Amy Duncan, Beth Evans-Ramos, and Lisa Hilderbrand

PHOTOGRAPHY BY
Kate Baldwin

SKIPSTONE

Cheers!

TRADER JOE'S®
SPECIALTY TEAS
Irish
Breakfast Tea
BAGGED TEA

NET WT 1.41 OZ (40g) - 20 TEA BAGS

dedication

To our customers, who have supported us,
inspired us, and befriended us.

contents

introduction

We started the Salvage Studio in 2004—three women unified by a lust for rust and a desire to adopt the mantra "reduce, reuse, recycle." Since then, we've devoted ourselves to rescuing abandoned, forgotten, or discarded items and then finding a new or better purpose for them, making castoffs into unique home, garden, and gift items.

Our studio is a place to gather ideas, collect supplies, foster creativity, and promote a sense of community. We've discovered that the energy and enthusiasm the three of us generate in our ecological and creative discoveries is contagious. Prompted by the belief that everyone has the capability to be expressive and might just need a nudge to get going, we offer workshops and demonstrations at our studio that captivate the mind and work the hands—all while using recycled materials that are readily available around us.

Each partner in the Studio has a unique approach to salvage-based projects, but we're consistent in our need to stay environmentally and ecologically focused.

Beth Evans-Ramos owns Garden Graces, a garden styling and decorating service that helps clients discover what colors and art can work in their gardens. Beth's

Vintage clocks with their worn faces and rusted mechanisms no longer keep time but have a graphic quality that reminds us of the need to slow down.

specialty creations include original furniture, mosaics, and decor made using found objects, cast-off treasures, and interesting salvage pieces. "My heart really belongs to the Salvage Studio these days," says Beth. "I'm amazed by how many fascinating people and wonderful new friends I've encountered as a result of the Studio." Amy and Lisa suspect, however, that Beth mostly enjoys having more reason to frequent thrift shops and estate sales, brake for free piles, and check out dumpsters.

—

(Left) Three lone metal chairs are united as a garden bench with the addition of a weathered barn board for a seat.
(Above) A rusted radiator is a perfect blue match to canning jars holding a spring bouquet.

Lisa Hilderbrand is a garden designer and educator who emphasizes earth-friendly gardening practices and low-maintenance gardens with year-round interest. Raised in eastern Washington in a very creative and resourceful family, Lisa learned at an early age to make do with what you have, which helped shape her ability to see objects in a new light. "I'm addicted to free piles and garage sales," she says, "and I always find treasures in others' trash! I love to decorate my home and garden with found objects." Lisa met Beth at a garden club, where they were both picking up a load of sword ferns for a plant sale. They quickly discovered a mutual love for shopping at Goodwill.

While studying economics and natural resource

management at the University of Wisconsin–Stevens Point, Amy Duncan removed everything from one wall of her dorm room to create an 8- by 7-foot collage, made up entirely of magazine ads. Over the years, she continued to indulge her artistic tendencies by tackling basket weaving, papermaking, textile construction, dressmaking, and vegetarian cooking. In 1999 she started Four Corners Design, a company that produces handcrafted greeting cards and decor using recycled materials combined into simple collages. Her hunt for interesting bits of flotsam to incorporate into her designs led her to stand in line for an estate sale—where she met Beth, who was also planning to make a beeline for the basement where all the "good stuff" was.

Eventually, the three of us amassed quite an accumulation of stuff, and we wanted to find a way to share our riches with others. Participating in one too many rainy outdoor weekend events convinced us that a permanent roof was necessary. We initially founded the Salvage Studio in a small, sublet location from which we operated one-day seasonal sales and a smattering of weekend workshops. The idea caught on immediately, to our delight but to the dismay of the landlord. So in 2006, we opened a new storefront location in Edmonds, a small community 20 miles north of Seattle. Our new, more spacious studio has plenty of room for visitors to browse displays (we call them "vignettes") showing our own projects, as well as workshop space for weekend classes, a resource library to stimulate creative thinking, and an outdoor patio dedicated to garden art and outdoor salvage.

It is our hope that this book will be a launching pad for your own ideas. To get you started, we've provided the particulars of how to construct some of our favorite projects, those that visitors find when they come to the Studio. But more importantly, we hope that this book can help you incorporate the concepts on which the Salvage Studio is based into your everyday life. The ability to use the materials at hand to make something that fills a need is present within all of us. The rhythm of our lives can be set by the choices we make every day. Home, family, earth, and community—these are what we hold dear. We hope our book encourages you to do the same.

(Left) Classic black and white is always a winner. The domino dots mimic the texture of the milk glass, and a collaged composition book becomes a journal for daily tasks, dreams, or doodles. (Right) An old picture frame is outfitted with fabric, ribbon, and upholstery tacks to make a message board. Scrabble tiles add words of advice.

recycle & reuse

Though "recycle" and "reuse" have recently become more popular in our current lingo, these ideas are hardly new. With the emergence of an environmental consciousness in the 1970s (I still vividly remember celebrating the first Earth Day), Beth, Lisa, and I each started on an eco-journey that would eventually lead us to cross paths and start the Salvage Studio.

The amount of "stuff" that is thrown away every day is astounding; we can only hope that the idea to tread more lightly on the planet moves from the current vogue to everyday practice. It seems that people throw away so much because they either can't think of alternative uses or don't take the time and effort to consider their consumption habits.

A perfect example of wanting to get rid of stuff but not knowing what to do with it occurred shortly after we created the Studio. Lisa's husband, Doug, grew up outside of Albany, Oregon, on a large farm. The farm had been idle for many years after Doug's father passed away and his mother entered a care facility. In preparation for family plans to sell the land, we traveled down to the farm to see what remained. Stuff was everywhere! From the rusting farm cultivators and combines laid to rest in overgrown fields to a henhouse past its

Castoffs combine for a favorite "vignette." At the Studio we use repeated colors, shapes, and scale to create an interesting story with the most common of objects.

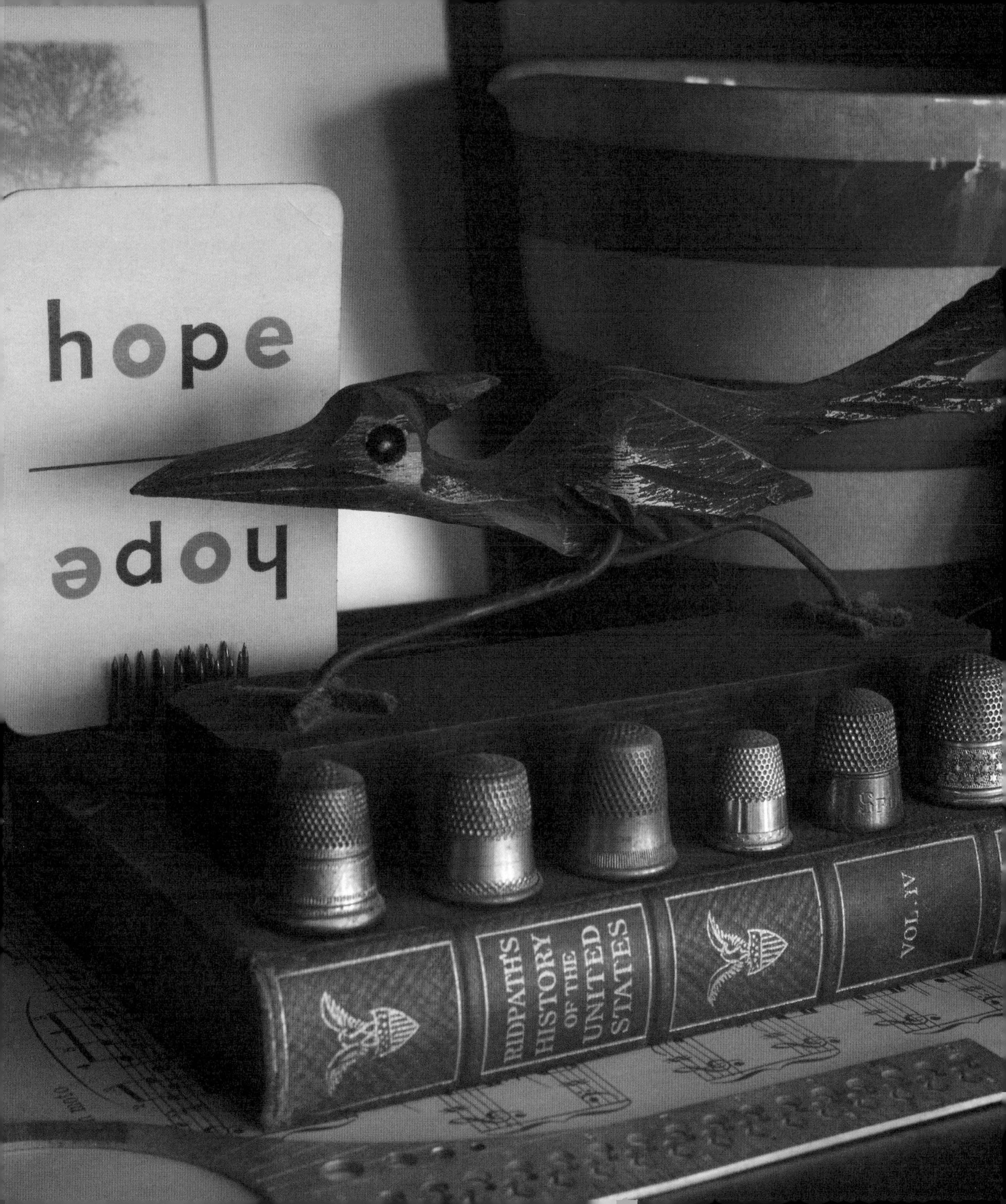
hope
hope
RIDPATH'S HISTORY OF THE UNITED STATES
VOL. IV

prime, the remnants of a prosperous life of a tinkerer and saver remained.

We spent two days scavenging among the piles, our brains constantly at work envisioning what new creations could emerge from our treasure trove. Doug's brothers initially thought we were two steps above trash pickers, but as we described how metal gears would become candlestick holders, a tractor seat would become an office

(Left) Metal scrap spells out "joy," while other metal gears, pans, springs, and tubing add interest to this outdoor setting. (Above) Metal gears from the Oregon farm comprise candleholders while discarded forks are turned into placecard holders.

chair, a gear box could be a patio umbrella stand, or a red metal grate could be a craft room organizer, they changed their thinking. They began pulling items out of the former workshop and offering their own suggestions of what each could be in its resurrected life. Given a new perspective on the possibilities of what lay before them, the brothers even found a few choice items that they deemed too good for us to haul away; they now had their own ideas. When we explained that the grain chute found in a twisted thicket would make a great garden waterfall, one of Lisa's sisters-in-law soundly agreed and claimed it as her own!

Sometimes a person can be overwhelmed by his or her stuff. After learning about us in the local press, a woman from Bellingham, Washington, contacted us. She was struggling with a house filled with a lifetime of clutter and memories. Her father, once a local art teacher, had moved into a nursing home. She felt that there were probably items in the house that would be useful to someone, but she just did not have the energy and stamina to deal with all of it. Before she had it all hauled off to the landfill, she wanted us to come and take a look. When we arrived, a few other family members were there, rummaging among the piles. We spent the day uncovering a healthy supply of art materials for our studio and hearing stories from fam-

ily members about their patriarch. It was a cathartic process for them—not only to physically get rid of some of the stuff, but to release themselves from their attachment to it.

The old adage "One man's trash is another man's treasure" has been borne out several times in our adventures in junking. What one person tosses, another gleans and puts to use. When we go yard-saling, my sister and I often hear people who are leaving as we arrive comment that they couldn't find anything they wanted

Spring brunch, Salvage Studio style!

to buy—and then we find abundant riches! It certainly holds true that everybody is looking for something different. One local charity group in my town, the Everett Assistance League, holds wonderful estate sales. My sister and I have become acquainted with several of the women who run these sales. I must have aroused their curiosity as I passed by the fine china and crystal in the living room and made a beeline for the garage or the basement to scrounge among the musty boxes of nuts and bolts, broken tools, or forgotten photographs. After they learned of the Salvage Studio and my work, the women became intrigued with what I was buying and what I might concoct with my purchases. They began to see the potential value in items that they had once considered to be worth mere pennies.

What to Look For

What is it, exactly, that we look for when scouring through a pile of junk? Everyone has their own personal favorites, those things that speak to them. I gravitate toward graphic items such as letters and numbers and anything of a scientific nature. Lisa has a fondness for the sweetness of a children's book or anything with a cat motif. Beth is drawn to vintage jewelry as well as rusty implements, whether it's an old enamelware pan that can be rejuvenated as a kitchen message board or a broken rake head that can be turned into a wall hook. For all three of us, a peely patina of paint or a corroded layer of rust is just the start of an inspirational groundswell. We know that such an item has been around for a while and has its own story to tell. Anything that has either a hole in the middle or one hole at each end holds endless possibilities: A hole in the middle means that it can be stacked or layered as a component in making a

---

Everyday Discards, Everyday Solutions

There are endless uses for the detritus left behind at yard sales. Here are a few quick ideas. Use an old cloth **measuring tape** as a funky ribbon to tie up a gift. A lone **saucer** can frame a favorite photograph; just trim the photo to a circular shape, adhere it to the indentation in the saucer, and hang it on the wall with a plate hanger. Colorful **cardboard boxes** from your favorite cereal can become a cover for a handmade journal. And the next time you find yourself without curtains, don't use the ubiquitous bed sheet as a temporary solution. Instead, tack a *National Geographic* **map** up by the corners. It will add much more color and interest to those bare windows.

---

new item; a hole on either end means it can be attached to a new creation with wire or screws.

What kinds of things do we leave behind? Anything that reeks of mold and mildew; those are strong adversaries not easily conquered. Since we deal with lots of metal pieces, we bypass anything with motor oil or any corrosive material on it. Anything of a toxic nature should be disposed of properly. (Check within your local community for disposal sites and regulations regarding hazardous materials.) Always be mindful of what you cannot use and how to get rid of it.

Figuring out how to use what others have tossed is both a challenge and a delight. Sometimes the original salvage idea doesn't translate into a practical application, in which case we don't feel too bad, since the materials were free or inexpensive to begin with. Some items have

How to Clean Your Newfound Treasures

Acquiring lots of great junk really is not a problem—the challenge is cleaning it up!

Needless to say, the junk we rescue does not arrive sparkling clean and ready to be used in craft projects. There is often quite a layer of dirt, grime, dust, and crud that we must remove before an object's true beauty is revealed.

Water is your greatest asset. If an item can withstand water, cleaning is much simplified. A spray hose, an old sponge, a sunny day, and a supply of elbow grease will help you make short work of removing accumulated debris from metal gears, wooden windows, garden tools, and wire baskets.

Kitchen cleanser. Most basic kitchen cleansers can be mixed with water to remove additional grime. Nonchlorine products, such as Bon Ami, are gentler on both the item being cleaned and the environment. Use a sponge with one sturdy scrubbing side, and wear a pair of rubber gloves.

An old toothbrush. Keep a few toothbrushes handy; they can get into crevices to clean out dirt.

Clean rags. Use clean towels or rags for wiping and drying.

Sandpaper. If you have an item that will not take well to water, such as a wooden chest or chair, sandpaper may be your best cleaning ally. Use a very fine grit (120 or 150 grit) and gently sand the surface, removing a fair amount of dirt while refreshing the finish. A final wipe with a damp rag will clean up the remaining debris.

---

simply lost their structural integrity over time. There have been occasions when I was cleaning up an item or attempting to attach it as part of a project and it fell apart or disintegrated. The tinkering that goes into the process of creating with salvaged objects is a surefire way to get your creative juices flowing. I like to challenge myself to discover new uses for those items that are a mainstay at thrift stores and garage sales: teacup saucers, old sporting trophies, worn-out measuring tapes, chipped dishes, and outdated *National Geographic* magazines.

Teacup saucers are often orphans, separated from their mates. The patterns can be lovely, and the small indentation for the teacup makes it ideal as a soap dish. Beth has discovered that a pretty saucer, holding a scented soap and tied up with a length of ribbon or tulle, makes a darling hostess gift. The small cup indentation is also the perfect size to hold a candle. Setting a saucer on your bedroom dresser to keep rings and earrings confined is another good recycled use.

Whenever we do a presentation at one of our local Goodwill stores, we always peruse the aisles for items to illustrate what can be done with what someone else has given up. As a result, every presentation is different because we never know what we might find. At one of our first Goodwill events, I came across a fine selection of old sport trophies, majestic metal figures of women with their arms outstretched. I incorporated them into a tabletop display that demonstrated how common objects can be displayed in uncommon ways. As I was returning the items to the store aisles after our presentation, I kept one of the trophies and purchased it for myself. Soon afterward I was struck with the notion to remake the golden goddess into a garden statuette, a Garden Goddess that could honor a favorite spot in my backyard. I immediately took the trophy apart and discovered that it was held together with a set of threaded screws and fasteners. Why couldn't I substitute quirky found metal pieces for the wooden base and plastic-coated pedestal? And why not incorporate garden items in the reconstruction process, like old flowerpots and hose nozzles? I find that once I light on an idea, my creativity is a powerful motivator. My sister and I spent several days acquiring more trophies, taking them apart, and collecting interesting metal pieces that either had a center hole or could be drilled for one, and then we concocted our creations. The result was a lively collection of Garden Goddesses, featuring the outstretched woman trophy figure as the pinnacle; Garden Guardians, using male statuettes; and Plant Trophies, using the eagles and star emblems that often embellish larger trophies. Whether you consider them trophies for a garden well maintained or a playful ode to Goodwill, the gold metal glints in the sunshine and they create a strange and delightful surprise amid the petals and foliage (see the Garden Goddess project).

I have always been fascinated by letters and numbers. Their graphic quality is so strong and immediate, and the combination of facts and figures appeals to my scientific side. I collect all sorts of things that measure—clocks, containers, calipers. Measuring tapes, broken, frayed, or worn, are always at the bottom of the barrel at a yard sale. I grab them up and receive the usual inquisitive look from the cashier, who is not quite

Two Garden Goddesses stand ready to honor the garden.

sure what good a broken measuring tape will do any-one. But I have found that these tapes, whether metal or cloth, make perfect borders. I finish off many of my original canvas collages by tacking measuring tape all around the outer edge. At our original Salvage Studio location, the bathroom had an odd two-tone combina-tion of paint, meeting horizontally at the halfway point on the wall, all around the room. I tacked a length of cloth measuring tape, taken from a rusted metal case, all around the room, covering the paint line between the two colors and making a salvage-style chair rail. Recycled upholstery tacks attached the tape to the wall; the visible inch measurements ensured even spacing of the tacks every 2 inches.

Old or damaged books and chipped dishes are two steadfast items that always find their way to the dump pile at a garage sale. Yet for me, each of these can be the foundation of a wonderful collage, defining new shapes, patterns, and combinations. I'm always fasci-nated by old books, especially reference volumes. Their yellowing pages, handsome illustrations, and anti-quated information intrigue me. Combining pages in which the words address a single theme but come from different sources is an interesting way to approach a decoupage tabletop. And when you use original pages, with their faded or yellowed patina, you create a work of art—instead of a cheap reproduction of vintage materials that you might find at a big craft store (see the Tabletop Collage project).

(Left) Old wooden skis, turned upside down and mounted on metal brackets, make a fine picture ledge. (Right) The Junker's Box from Beth's car.

Turning broken and chipped dishes into ceramic mosaics is certainly not a new idea. But given the response to various mosaic classes we give regularly at the Salvage Studio, it is very popular! The opportunity to save that treasured but now cracked teacup or special serving dish resonates with people. My sister Stacey wanted to add sev-eral stepping-stones to the backyard garden. The mosaic idea appealed to her, but she wanted a project that was easy to complete and not too cumbersome. She bought several concrete pavers at the local home improvement store, making sure they were dry and free of moisture, and sealed each of them with a coat of diluted white glue. She then composed a mosaic design on top of each paver,

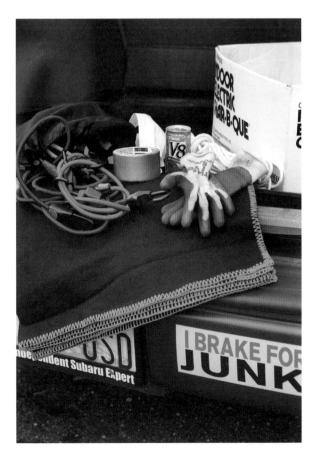

gluing the broken dish pieces to the paver with an outdoor adhesive (she used Loctite Power Grab). After all the pieces were in place, she used tile grout to finish the top and let it dry completely. She sealed the completed piece with grout sealer because the pavers would be outside in the garden and she wanted them to withstand moisture and changes in temperature. We now have the most beautiful pavers made from dishes otherwise destined for the dump.

You have to give credit to the people at *National Geographic*; not only have they managed to get practically everyone on earth to subscribe to their magazine, but they have imbued the publication with such value that it seems sacrilegious to throw an issue away. Certainly the photography is amazing, and you do learn about places and people you never knew much about. But there has to be a greater use beyond taking up space on a bookshelf. One idea is to turn those beautiful photographs into envelopes. It's easy to do: Gently pull apart an existing envelope you have at home for a pattern, lay it on top of the photograph, trace along the edge, cut it out, and then glue the sides together so the desired photo faces out. Write a letter to a friend, send a note to your mother, or pay a bill and then mail it off in the photo envelope. Whoever receives it on the other end is sure to smile.

On a similar note, I often send postcards to friends with just a quick line to let them know I am thinking of them. The cardboard boxes that contain your morning cereal, the bathroom tissue, or your frozen dinner have colorful graphics and eye-catching appeal when trimmed to a 4- by 6-inch postcard size. On the blank side, you can write your brief note on half, add the address and postage on the other half, and then drop it in the mailbox to brighten someone else's day.

Free Stuff

While you are out running errands, develop an eye for free piles. A "free pile" is a discarded heap on the side of the road or in front of someone's house that has been left out in the hope that it will attract attention. It takes a trained eye to spot such a pile and dexterity to safely pull off the road and maneuver your way back to it, so you can discern whether there is anything of value to take. Lisa is the expert here—not only can she spot a free pile from a considerable distance, but she can determine in a moment's glance whether there is anything of value worth stopping for. If space permits, have your Junker's Box (see "The Junker's Box") in the car at all times. At the very least, always keep a tape measure in your purse or car and a few bungee cords and an old bath towel in your trunk. When opportunity presents itself, you just might find that perfect entryway table hidden in the beaten frame of an old wooden dresser or a set of backyard wind chimes disguised as the remnants of a child's swing set.

In addition to finding fortuitous items on the side of the road, there are other great sources of free stuff. Craigslist and freecycle.com are two of the most popular online venues, but be forewarned: free items go fast! Your local newspaper may also be a place to look for free merchandise. My newspaper has a daily classified section for free items that I can opt to have emailed to me. Since most newspapers now have their classifieds online, it's become amazingly simple to use the search function to find the free stuff—and you don't even have to pull over!

———

A discarded mailbox becomes a planter for a container garden. Remember to drill holes in the bottom of the mailbox for sufficient drainage.

Chair-Springs Candle Chandelier

A tossed seat from a broken chair has little use in its original form. But the curvature of the chair springs can hold a set of glass votive holders, giving you a salvage chandelier anywhere you want to hang some soft candlelight. We actually used a donated collection of large test tubes with tapers inside instead of votives, but the coiled springs will conform to and hold a variety of glass sizes. Standard votive holders are 2½ inches high and will work fine for this project. If your springs are larger, you might also try pint canning jars.

The size of the section of coiled springs will vary, depending upon what you find, but the one we used is about average. In addition to chair springs, springs from an old baby crib mattress work particularly well, as the wire is usually of a light gauge and easy to cut. Coils from a bed box spring can also work for this project.

Materials:

- Discarded chair seat spring, approximately 16 by 18 by 3 inches
- 4 equal lengths of heavy twine or medium-weight chain, each approximately 48 inches long
- Large S hook at least 1½ inches long
- 6 to 12 glass votive holders, depending upon the size of your spring section and how elaborate you want your final chandelier to be
- 1 votive candle for each glass holder

Tools:

- Lineman's pliers
- Scissors
- Wire cutters

1. Remove all padding and debris from the chair seat spring. The padding is usually attached either with large staples or tied on with twine. The staples can be removed with the lineman's pliers and the twine cut with scissors. The springs are usually all connected to form a square. Using your wire cutters, clip off any stray coil pieces that poke outside the square border. If you are using bed springs rather than chair seat springs, you will need to use the wire cutters to cut a section of springs the size of your desired chandelier.

Candlelight from the Chair-Springs Candle Chandelier creates a soothing atmosphere for a warm bath. Tall glass votives collaged with vintage paper ephemera add to the ambience.

A square shape works best, with either 9 springs (3 rows of 3 springs) or 16 springs (4 rows of 4 springs). Use the lineman's pliers to bend back any cut wire edges so they don't snag.

2. Determine the top side of the chandelier. Springs usually spiral in a funnel form, with the top of the spiral larger than the bottom. You want to use this spiral to your advantage, so have the wide end of the funnel shape up. That way, you can insert the glass votive holders into the spirals and have the narrowing of the spirals hold them in place.

3. Attach each piece of twine or chain to one corner. If you are using heavy twine, tie each piece on, ensuring that the tail end is not so long as to be burned by a lit votive. If you are using chain, open the last link of chain, link it around the corner wire, and close it up with the lineman's pliers. Gather up the ends of the twine or chain and bring them together, centering them over the top of the springs and fastening all four ends to the S hook. If using chain, you can simply slip the hook through each of the four ending links. If using twine, knot the four ends together, about 3 inches down from where the ends meet. Then slip the knot around the S hook.

4. Your chandelier is now ready to hang—either from a tree branch in your yard for al fresco dining or from a secured ceiling hook in your house.

5. Arrange your glass votive holders in the coils in any pattern you wish. Insert a votive candle into each glass holder and light—voilá!

Wire and twine are uncommon elements for a bathroom chandelier, while a narrow pine box, turned upside down and attached to the wall as a shelf, adds another unexpected salvage detail.

Tabletop Collage

Damaged books are one of the most common items that are disposed of, their owners no longer finding use for them. An appealing color or finish of paper, combined with expressive or beautiful fonts, can impart a stunning graphic quality to a plain table. I often adopt a theme when designing a tabletop, which helps me with page selection. Draw inspiration from the room the table will be in (cozy den, children's playroom, plant-filled sunroom) or from what it will be used for (reading glasses, flower vase, family photographs). Choose book pages that feature words, phrases, titles, imagery, and font styles that complement the room or intended use, or select pages that have a variety of different texts and sizes.

Wooden tables are easiest to work with, since the glue readily adheres to the surface. Start with a smaller side table; once you have the basic decoupage technique down, you can progress to larger surfaces with confidence.

Garden flowers mimic the graphic design used in this collage tabletop.

Materials:

- 8 to 10 pages from a standard-size 8½- by 11-inch book, or 12 to 15 pages from a 5½- by 8½-inch book
- Small wooden side table, with top approximately 16 by 20 inches
- Basic white school glue, such as Elmer's or any PVA (polyvinyl acetate) glue

- Paste wax, such as Johnson's

Tools:

- 8½- by 11-inch sheet of fine-grit (100 or 120) sand-paper
- Small plastic mixing container, such as a washed-out yogurt or cottage cheese cup

- Rectangular plastic dishwashing tub
- 2-inch chip brush
- Supply of soft rags

1. Begin by collecting your book pages. You may want to slightly overlap pages or tear the pages into smaller pieces to fit your tabletop. Do a dry run of your layout

Old Nails in the Garage

At estate sales, you'll often find the best bargains out in the garage. Not only are there spools of wire and broken tape measures, each of which is salvage-crafting gold, but you'll most likely also find coffee cans or jars of nails and screws at rock-bottom prices. Almost every project we put together or every item we repair needs an odd nail or screw. Our parents and grandparents didn't just pop into the car and head for the nearest megahardware store to buy a box of nails. They went out to their garage or shop, looked in their can of nails, and grabbed the one that would work the best. That is how it should be done! I love to use up what I have on hand and make it work. And a great side benefit we have found is that old metal is strong metal. Older screws don't get their heads stripped as easily when you torque down on them with a screwdriver. Older nails drive straighter and quicker, and the heads don't buckle when you try to pull them out with a hammer.

When Lisa was a child, the school district tore down the junior high building that was across the street from her house. They let people come in ahead of time to salvage wood, bricks, and other fixtures. Of course, her family was right there in the thick of things. Her brother cleaned mortar off bricks for the construction company to earn spending money. Her parents salvaged pine boards from the interior of the school walls. And most of the nails they pulled from the wood came out straight and true. (Her father even managed to straighten the bent ones with a hammer for reuse.)

With the wood they salvaged, they built a deck off the back of their house that was 22 feet by 11 feet—with nary a knot in it. The nails they pulled out and straightened held it together. They also built a brick patio on the ground level off to the side, using extra bricks from her brother's job.

So on your next estate-sale excursion, head for the garage, and don't overlook those forgotten tins of nails.

---

before you glue the paper down. It is easier to make adjustments in your design without worrying about the glue drying. Also think about changing the orientation of some pages; turn pages on their side or use just a portion of text to add visual interest.

A thin piece of plywood, cut to size and decoupaged with dictionary and encyclopedia pages, enlivens this metal frame patio table missing its glass top. A vintage canning jar with its decorative circle of stars holds a refreshing beverage.

2. Prepare the surface of the table by cleaning it thoroughly, letting it dry, and then sanding it. Sanding will prepare the surface to receive the glue and allow for greater adhesion.

3. In the small mixing container, prepare a solution of 2 parts glue to 1 part water. A total of 1 cup of this solution should be plenty for a small tabletop.

4. Put your collected book pages in the plastic dishwashing tub that has been filled halfway with warm

water. The warm water will soften the pages and make them more pliable, easier to work with, and more receptive to the glue mixture. Let the pages soak for 5 to 10 minutes.

5. With your chip brush, paint a section of the table with the glue/water mixture. Lay down one of your wet book pages, positioning it where you would like it to be. Brush the page with a light coating of the glue/water mixture, making sure no air bubbles are trapped underneath. Continue covering the rest of the tabletop in this manner with your book pages. When you are finished, let it dry completely, 24 to 48 hours.

6. Once your tabletop is dry, lightly sand the top and the edges. This will smooth out your surface and also give it a well-worn look. Wipe off any sanding residue with a dry rag.

7. Using a soft, clean rag, apply a light coat of paste wax to the surface. Let the wax dry for 15 to 20 minutes and then buff with another soft, clean rag. You can continue to add more wax, depending upon the sheen you desire. The wax will protect the tabletop and cause water spills to bead up. For a more durable finish, substitute polyurethane sealer for the wax.

Garden Goddess

Trophies from long-forgotten accomplishments are common at thrift stores. Funky art made from a trophy figurine and other random metal pieces becomes a stellar award for your garden. Metal trophies are more durable and weather resistant, but the gold-painted molded plastic versions will work too. I named these treasures Garden Goddesses because I used the figure of Victory with her arms outstretched. To give more of a garden feel to a finished goddess, you might use a metal flower frog or garden hose nozzle for one of the middle components. You can also use the trophy top that portrays a stately man with his arms crossed over his chest; I like to call this version the Garden Guardian. But you can use any trophy figure or other materials that you like; there is no prescribed set of instructions—just the reward of your creativity.

Materials:

- 1 or 2 discarded trophies
- Assorted metal and ceramic odds and ends—anything from a flowerpot to a pot grate to an old circular saw blade will work, as long as there is a center

Garden Goddesses, composed of trophy tops, rusted metal washers, a garden nozzle, and a steamer insert, stand ready to pay homage to a blooming plant.

The Junker's Box

It's very handy to have the necessary equipment for a spur-of-the-moment salvaging opportunity. Our theory is that the nicer you are dressed, the better your chances of finding a swell pile of free rusty, muddy treasures. Beth keeps her junker's box in the back of her Subaru at all times. It doesn't have to be a box; any bag, bucket, or basket will do. Or you can be like Amy and simply keep the bare necessities loose behind the driver's seat of your car. Here's our list of what to include:

Gloves. Our favorites are garden gloves that have vinyl coating over the fingers and palms, such as Atlas gloves.

A **blanket** or **mattress pad** for protecting your car and/or your finds.

Bungee cords in various sizes. Buy the deluxe kind. We see too many dead bungee cords on the roadside.

Antibacterial wipes and/or **gel**. (There are even lovely scented ones that make the perfect hostess gift for your fellow junking friends and family.)

Disposable air masks. You've read about the danger of mold, but also consider lingering fumes from a house fire or cigarette smoke, rodent droppings, and years of accumulated dust. When you hit an estate sale or auction, a little protection is useful. (Beth wears glasses and has found that the flat face masks your dentist wears don't steam them up as readily as other kinds. Our local Costco for business customers sells boxes of them at very reasonable prices.)

Extra **cloth tote bags.** They are a staple in free boxes at garage sales and come in handy for wrapping small things.

Bottle of water, for drinking and/or washing.

Can of V-8 Juice, or some other healthy pick-me-up, for when your foraging takes longer than you expected. When you are finding treasure after treasure and are nowhere near a fine dining establishment, V-8 and cheese sticks can hit the spot.

Something red—a bandana, plastic tape, or cloth that is brightly colored red, orange, yellow, or pink—for marking the end of an object hanging out too far from the back of your car or truck.

Duct tape. Need we say more?

Vinyl apron, to protect your outfit when that "free" sign lures you to the side of road and you'd like to arrive at your destination without a rusty midriff.

If you drive a truck, include a **plastic tarp** to secure your load. And for a real touch of convenience, get the Spyder. It is a spiderweb made of bungee cords with hooks on the corners and sides. We received ours from Marie, the lovely woman mentioned in the Look chapter, and we have warm, fuzzy thoughts of her every time we use it because it works so well and saves us a ton of time.

Another suggestion is to keep a hidden cache of **money** somewhere in your car for unexpected hot estate sales. Or for when you need to pay for something boring, like a tank of gas. Wash out a small, empty, opaque hand lotion bottle, and store some cash inside.

hole or you can drill a center hole in it

- Assorted hex nuts
- Assorted metal fender washers

Tools:

- Hand-held power drill with bits in assorted sizes, if drilling is needed
- Hammer, if drilling is needed
- Center punch or nail, if drilling is needed
- Safety goggles, if drilling is needed
- Lineman's pliers
- Needle-nose pliers

1. Begin by dismantling your trophy. Most trophies screw apart, which can be accomplished by loosening the hex nut on the bottom of the base. After you have disassembled the trophy, you will be left with several parts. Save all the threaded rods, the hex nuts, and the threaded connectors; you will use these pieces to reconstruct your Garden Goddess (or Garden Guardian as the case may be!).

2. The top of your goddess will be the trophy top; the bottom of the goddess needs to be the largest and heaviest component of your creation. I have used overturned flowerpots, metal lampshades, and an enamelware colander as bases. Pick your base from your collected odds and ends.

3. Once you have determined the top and the bottom, whatever goes in the middle is up to you. I've used metal globes, doorknob backplates, the outside casing of a garden hose nozzle, and an old funnel. It really becomes a trial-and-error process, trying one piece out and then another until you find a pleasing combination and satisfactory fit. If you have an interesting piece that you would like to incorporate into your design and it is lacking a center hole, drill a hole with a power drill. With a hammer and a center punch or nail, make a small dimple where you would like to drill the hole. This will prevent the drill bit from skipping when you begin to drill. Wearing safety goggles, drill your hole, making sure it is large enough to fit the existing threaded rod. See "Drilling Silver Plate" in the Look chapter for more information about drilling metal.

4. The length of the threaded rod you have (from dismantling the original trophy) will dictate how tall your finished goddess will be. If you desire a taller goddess, purchase a longer threaded rod at the hardware store. You will reuse the threaded connector that originally connected the trophy top to the base of the trophy for this same purpose. To ensure that all your component pieces fit tightly, use additional hex nuts and fender washers for stability.

5. Once you have decided on the order of the parts, you are ready to complete your goddess. The goddess will be on top, with the trophy connector at her base, attached to the threaded rod. Thread your other bits and bobs onto the rod. Finally, thread the rod through the base and secure the bottom of the rod with a fender washer and hex nut. Gradually tighten the hex nut, keeping all of the component pieces in alignment. Your goddess is now ready to grace your garden.

begin

The morning brings with it not only a sense of newness and anticipation of the day ahead, but also the expectation of continued routines that lend a rhythm and reason to our daily life and provide a framework in which to take on unplanned adventures.

I find mornings the perfect time to have a ritual that eases me into the day and all the activity, commotion, stress, and excitement that will follow. The quietness of the morning is ideal for renewing myself and planning

Bolsters made from wool blankets, family photos, and fresh flowers in silver-plated vases add to this cozy atmosphere. Vintage volumes provide color and texture as well as raise the reading lamp.

for the day ahead. Waking at generally the same time every morning is a practice I have employed for many years—it keeps my body on a consistent clock. My awakening often begins with a whiff of subtle fragrance. I keep a small bouquet of flowers on my bedside table in a tarnished silver-plated vase that I found at a yard sale several years ago. I love including a sprig or two of rosemary; in the Northwest, rosemary grows year-round and is an earthy addition to any bouquet.

My love for silver plate extends beyond my bedside vase. All three of us at the Salvage Studio have a great affinity for silver plate. The variety of shapes and sizes and uses, from vases to bowls to platters, adds interest to any item you use them for. And we never bother with

Old Blanket Bolsters

Bolster pillows are useful if you read in bed and want extra support for your lower back. All you need is an old blanket and two leather belts, preferably the same width and color. A queen-size blanket will yield a larger, fatter bolster, while a twin size will offer a more petite version. If your blanket is made of wool and is dirty, you can clean it in the washing machine. Use cold water and a delicate cycle. The blanket may shrink, but it also will be softened—perfect for its reinvented use as a bolster. Once your blanket is clean, roll it up just as you would roll up a sleeping bag. I usually fold the edges to the inside so it has a nice finished look. After it is rolled, bind up the blanket with the two leather belts, one cinched on each end. The diameter of the bolster is usually smaller than the size of the belt. On the inside of the leather, mark the location where you want the belt to close. Then make a new belt hole with a hammer and awl. Do the same for the other belt. Trim off the end of each belt so that they are the same length. Cinch up your bolster, secure each belt, and you are finished. Don't have two leather belts? Substitute two straps from a shoulder bag or a decorative curtain tieback; tie the latter in a square knot to hold the bolster securely.

polishing! The patina that develops over time only adds to its character. A generation ago, so many women packed away these metal treasures, bringing them out just for special occasions. The time and energy (to say nothing of the chemicals) used to keep them sparkling were tremendous. We want to enjoy their beauty every day and not worry about the tarnish. It doesn't affect their use as decorative and organizational items, and since they are metal, they are sturdy and virtually indestructible.

Before rousing myself from bed in the morning, I like to lie there for a few minutes and savor its comfort. There are plenty of thrifty ideas for making your bed a comfort zone. The designer look of voluptuous linens and pillows is easy to attain. Start by limiting your bedroom color palette to just one major color with just one accent color. As you scour the thrift store, look for sheets, pillowcases, shams, and throws in your major color only. Use your one accent color as the determining factor in whether an item is a match. Patterns do not have to repeat; in fact, the key to the designer look is a combination of florals with stripes, plaids, or geometrics. It is the color consistency that ties the look together. If you find bedding linens in good shape, you can use them as is. If they have signs of wear but the color or pattern is right, use them to make reinvented throw pillows, coverlets, or other bedroom accessories.

For my own bedroom, I made a duvet cover from a floral damask king sheet sewn to a king floral coverlet, both of which I found at Goodwill. Using a king-size duvet or comforter on a queen size bed (and likewise a queen-size comforter on a double bed) will provide an overhang of comforter over the side of the bed and add to a feeling of fullness. You can easily make an attractive bed skirt simply by draping a double-size vintage bedspread over the box spring. The center of the bed-spread might be worn and stained, but that doesn't matter, since only the portion about 15 inches around the perimeter of the bedspread shows. A bedroom throw for my reading chair was originally a large tablecloth, and the bed bolsters are made from old blankets. It all works together because I am consistent about staying within my bedroom color scheme of tan (my primary color) with cranberry (my accent color).

———

Silver-plated creamers, glass carafes, and ironstone platters find new use in the bathroom.

Bath Time

You can start your day in a bathroom filled with repurposed objects. Almost anything can be used as a soap dish and will offer much more personality than a store-bought version. Lovely lone ironstone saucers multiply at the thrift stores and are the perfect size for a round of soap. Pressed glass and well-loved silver-plated trays are two other options. Creamers and sugar bowls, also in glass, china, or silver plate, can offer tidy solutions in the bath—use them to store cotton swabs, cotton balls, lipsticks, small soaps, hair clips, or Band-Aids. An interesting single drinking glass can hold toothbrushes or collect tweezers, scissors, and nail clippers all in one container.

Glass decanters that once held scotch or bourbon can now hold mouthwash, bath oil, or foaming bubble bath.

A giant reclaimed wicker laundry basket holds rolls and rolls of white toilet paper in my bathroom. Since I have no bathroom closet, I needed some practical storage solutions that still look good. The smooth white rolls contrast with the rough brown willow for a pleasing effect—and there is always plenty of toilet paper at hand. An old milking stool is conveniently placed next to my toilet for the current toilet paper roll, while an old scale is now employed to hold a stack of hand towels. Wire baskets hold our other bathroom sundries while offering additional texture to the mix. Cotton pillowcases are given new life by being stitched into laundry bags. Hang a different bag for each family member on accessible hooks or knobs, or use different bags to sort dirty laundry into whites, colors, and towels. The sorting will then be done when it is time to wash. (See the Pillowcase Laundry Bags project.)

The potential for clutter in any bathroom, with its plethora of lotions, creams, pastes, gadgets, and tools, is great. One of the best ways I have found to keep the top of my bathroom vanity tidy is to organize these receptacles on an ironstone platter. Placing dissimilar items on a platter instantly provides neatness and order, since everything is collected together in one place.

Wooden picture frames can also be put to good salvage use in either the bath or the bedroom or wherever you dress for the day. A wooden frame with its glass front intact can be made into a dresser tray to keep your vanity clutter under control. Insert a piece of wallpaper or other decorative paper into the frame so that its decorative side faces out against the glass. Attach a firm piece of cardboard to the back of the frame with carpentry staples. Adhere a small felt or cork dot to each back corner of the frame so it doesn't scratch the vanity top. Turn the frame right side up and you have an ideal spot to corral earrings, lipsticks, or perfume bottles.

Another use for a picture frame is as an upright jewelry holder. Replace the glass with a piece of metal window screening, cut to extend just beyond the inside edge

Salvage Definition: Ironstone

A favorite at the Salvage Studio, ironstone is a type of dense, durable stoneware first introduced in the early 19th century by English potters. The creamy white pottery was designed as a cheaper substitute for porcelain and sold primarily in the United States, where it was much more popular than in England. The simple lines and shapes, as well as its durability, led to its widespread use. Since several English potters and later many American suppliers mass-produced everything from plates to bowls to pitchers in this sturdy ceramic, it is readily found and appreciated by collectors today.

You can often find lovely old ironstone with nicks, chips, and cracks at estate sales. Though these well-loved pieces are no longer appropriate for serving food, they can still be used as decorative objects—a platter in the bath to hold bottles, a creamer on a windowsill to hold a bouquet, a teacup at your desk to hold paper clips.

The day begins with breakfast in the kitchen and Calvin eager for his morning walk. The kitchen island is made of recycled wood and is the workhorse of the house.

of the frame. Secure the screen with staples to the back of the frame. Attach two eyehooks along opposite sides of the frame for threading a decorative ribbon through the eyehooks and hanging on the wall. You now have a marvelous location to keep earrings and necklaces.

Kitchen Confidential

The rituals of walking the dog, collecting the newspaper, and starting the coffeemaker lend cadence to the early morning. I love drinking from vintage diner mugs, with their creamy heft that retains the heat of the brew. It took hardly any time at all to collect a set of 12 mugs from visits to nearby thrift stores. In the same fashion, I likewise acquired cereal bowls and small plates, all of the same age, hue, and sturdiness. Mismatched silverware, plaid dish towels refolded as napkins, and vintage jelly-jar juice glasses complete the breakfast table.

My kitchen island, a handsome wooden piece built from reclaimed lumber and painted molding, is the workhorse of the kitchen. This island is my mainstay, from morning breakfast to afternoon art projects to dinner preparation. To keep the top looking good, I use a heavy cotton woven throw rug as a table runner. The sturdy weave stands up to constant use, and it can easily be washed in the washing machine. Rag rugs in a cacophony of colors are frequent finds at yard sales, and they are perfect for this use. As much I as try to use cloth napkins and woven dish towels, since they can be washed

and used over and over again, a roll of paper towels is always standing by. A paper towel holder made from 5-pound disc weights and a long metal auger gives that salvage touch to the kitchen (see the Auger or Spindle Paper-Towel Holder project).

Reusing glass canning jars for storing grains, flours, sugar, and coffee in the kitchen is an old idea that continues to make good sense. Purchasing these food staples in bulk eliminates excessive packaging, and the glass jars make it easy to view the contents. Metal baskets of every size and shape help to organize kitchen staples and round up counter sundries. You can also attach baskets to the wall, keeping items close at hand while freeing up counter work area.

A towel shelf is a clever use for a discarded tool caddy. Turned upside down, the former insert for a metal toolbox can do double duty, with a storage shelf on top and a small towel bar below (see the Tool-Caddy Towel Rack project).

The one recycled item that is absolutely indispensable in my kitchen is the blackboard, a large wood-framed piece that dominates one wall. This standard schoolroom icon can often be found at thrift stores or salvage shops. Even if you can't find a vintage blackboard to mount, you can make your own. Blackboard paint is now available at most hardware stores. Tape off a portion of your wall, prime and paint the area with the blackboard paint, and then frame the area with wooden molding for a custom design. Messages from other fam-

A rusted birdcage holds a dried bouquet memento. A worn table, refreshed with a coat of creamy paint, is the gathering spot for toiletries and sundries in vintage silver-plated and glass containers.

Repairing Chips in Ceramics

Here's a quick tip for repairing chips and nicks on the rim of worn ceramic dishes. The repaired platter will not be safe for food use, but its sharp edges will be eliminated, so it can serve a new life as an organizing platter in the bath or on top of your dresser. Using a small square of 60-grit sandpaper, gently sand away the rough edges around the outside of the chip. Once the edges are smoothed, continue to sand the chip to make it as even as possible with the rest of the rim. When you are finished sanding, wipe away any dust residue. Cover the sanded area with a light coat of clear nail polish; this will restore the sheen to the sanded area and make it less conspicuous within the glazed finish.

ily members, reminders of appointments, and shopping lists can be contained in one location, without pesky paper notes accumulating and invariably getting lost or tossed. Two cup hooks attached to the bottom of the wooden frame keep track of spare car and house keys.

Window Dressing

While I love using dish towels as oversize napkins, printed dish towels and tea towels can also make charming café curtains in the kitchen. Hung on a metal café rod with clip curtain rings, the towels can grace the lower pane of a kitchen window. Using such simple mechanics, you can change your curtains with each season.

Hooks, Handles, and Knobs

Ideas for hooks and handles escalate when using junk—almost anything can be made into a handle or a hook. While home improvement stores have hooks and handles in every size, shape, and color imaginable, creating your own will give you a unique look at an affordable price. I have found that hooks and knobs are one of the easiest ways to hang up items, keeping them off the floor and organized. In my turn-of-the-century home, closets are practically nonexistent. Though a previous remodel did add two closets to the upstairs bedrooms, on the main floor of the house such amenities are lacking. I've used salvaged hooks and knobs to not only add a special touch but also provide the storage and organization that every home needs. In the guest bathroom, I attached seven old **steel hooks** to a strip of peeling painted molding and attached this molding along one entire length of the bathroom wall. It provides more room for bath towels (hanging right over the heating grate so they dry quickly) and guests belongings than a rod would, and the two hooks at the far end of the molding extend over the vanity—well suited for a hand towel and a decorative hanging picture.

In the master bath, which didn't have towel bars, I employed a similar technique. In this case, I dressed up the hooks, since the master bath has a more clean-lined look. Using a piece of **scrap lumber** as my base, I attached a corner rosette to each end. These rosettes are readily available at lumber stores; I chose a style that matched the rest of the molding in the room. I then sanded and painted the entire piece the same white color as the wall and lined it with matching chrome hooks, spacing them evenly. **Salvaged metal doorstops** could easily be substituted for store-bought hooks. They are sturdy, come in a variety of finishes (brass, chrome, white, and black), and easily attach to a length of molding or scrap lumber. In fact, you can use as a hook almost any rigid metal scrap that forms an angle. Outside in my garden, I've resurrected a single **metal shelf bracket** with decorative flourishes and a lovely patina as a planter hook. Without its mate, the bracket is worthless for its original purpose but is reborn when given a new use. Firmly attached to a fence post on one end, the screw hole in the other end is perfect for the hook of a hanging basket, allowing the basket chain sufficient distance from the fence to hang freely.

Anything that has a hole in it or can have a hole drilled into it can function as a knob or handle. I acquired a worn black dresser that I turned into a buffet in my dining room. After sanding and waxing the surface, I needed to figure out handles for the drawers. Since I collect sewing paraphernalia, I had several **metal sewing bobbins.** Using fender washers and threaded spacers, I attached the bobbins to the drawer, using the holes from the previous knobs. If you don't have sewing bobbins, wooden **thread spools,** round **Tinkertoy parts,** or garden **faucet handles** are all good substitutes. Depending on the function and style of the piece, anything is possible. If you have two holes on a drawer or cabinet front, reminders of a previous handle, you can thread decorative **ribbon** or braid through the holes and knot off the ends to make a very casual pull.

At the Salvage Studio, the kitchen cabinets were plain and poorly finished, with paint that was chipped and worn. After decoupaging the outside face of each cabinet, I finished them off with **silverware handles.** To make these, drill two holes in an old spoon—one in the middle of the bowl of the spoon and the other through the spoon's end—then attach the spoon handle to the cabinet door, using screws and plastic spacers. The spacers should be long enough to allow a hand to slip through and grab the handle. (For more information, see the Silverware Handles and Pulls project in the Look chapter.)

And what to do with **orphaned knobs?** Use a hanger bolt—a specialty screw with one end for screwing into metal (your orphaned knob) and the other end for screwing into the wall—and you can have a decorative picture hanger that adds class and style to the simplest picture or mirror.

Vintage dish towels will lend a salvage touch to your window, but often these well-loved linens are not in pristine condition. With some effort, you can remove or at least diminish minor stains. Begin by soaking the linens in water at room temperature for a day or two; old linen fibers can be dry from lack of recent use. Once the fibers are pliable, you can use one of the enzyme presoaks or oxygen bleaches to remove stains. Stay away from chlorine bleach, which is too harsh for these older fibers and will weaken and shred them. The old standby of lemon juice, dabbed on the stain and then dried in direct sunlight, also can bleach away light stains without the use of harsh chemicals.

These easy curtains work just as well in the bathroom. Instead of dish towels, use lace tablecloths, embroidered linen hand towels, or even pretty floral scarves. The metal café rod with clip-on rings is easy and convenient, but other choices include tree branches, which lend a graceful arch, or a discarded wooden broom handle for a more rustic feel. Creative window treatments can be used throughout the house. Hanging drapes in the living room, dining room, or bedroom may call for a more substantial approach, and in my quest for cost-effective curtain rods, I came upon bamboo poles from the local garden center. These poles, approximately 1 to 1½ inches in diameter, are a perfect solution. With a bit of ingenuity, I fashioned curtain rods at a fraction of the cost of commercial rods. This money-saving method allowed me to spend more on the natural-weave linen panels I wanted. The pairing of the bamboo rod with the linen is a clean-lined approach that ties together the rooms in my house with a coordinated look.

Pillowcase Laundry Bags

Mismatched pillowcases proliferate at the thrift store. Find two or three matching patterns and colors and you'll have a coordinated look for stowing dirty clothes. Look for pillowcases that are constructed with the hem at the open end sewn *after* the side seam was sewn. This will allow you to easily insert the drawstring.

Materials:
- Cotton pillowcase
- Thread to match pillowcase
- About 2 yards ribbon or cording for the drawstring

Tools:
- Sewing machine
- Seam ripper or small sewing scissors
- Safety pin

1. Stitch the casing for the drawstring. First, sew one row of straight stitching approximately 2 inches below the top of the pillowcase, encircling the entire hem in an even line. Use your machine's seam width gauge to guide your stitching.

2. Sew an identical row 1 inch below the first stitching and 3 inches from the top of the pillowcase, again encircling the entire hem.

3. In the side seam, make a ½-inch-wide slit, between the two rows of stitching. This is most easily accomplished by gently opening the seam using a seam ripper or small sewing scissors.

4. Tack a small stitch at each end of the slit for reinforcement.

5. Thread your drawstring through the newly stitched channel, using a safety pin hooked to one end of the drawstring as your guide. Use a coordinated length of ribbon or cording or even a lone shoelace as your

A trio of pillowcase laundry bags hangs from a bath-towel rack made from scrap lumber and metal schoolhouse hooks .

drawstring. Once you have pulled your drawstring through, continue pulling it until the loose ends are even. Knot the ends together 1 inch from the end; this will ensure that the drawstring does not get pulled out when you open up the laundry bag.

Tool-Caddy Towel Rack

The insert tray to a metal toolbox is often separated from its mate. At yard or estate sales where there is a garage or basement filled with tools, you are likely to find both metal toolboxes and their insert trays. On their own, these trays make great organizers in the office or kitchen. Inspiration for another use struck one day when I turned a toolbox tray upside down. Mounted to the wall, it can provide a small shelf with a horizontal towel bar underneath. This rustic metal look is at home in the kitchen, bath, or garden shed. If you don't have a tool caddy, you can turn any shallow wooden box upside down and attach it to the wall for a simple shelf. An old garden trug with a carrying handle is ideal.

Materials:
- Metal toolbox tray
- 2 wall anchors with their accompanying screws (choose a size based on how you plan to use your shelf; wall anchors have a load limit listed on the package)
- 2 washers to fit around the screws

Tools:
- Ruler
- Pencil
- Hammer
- Center punch or 3-inch nail
- Hand-held power drill
- Drill bits equal to the diameter of your screws
- Level

1. Measure and mark the positions for two equally spaced holes, one on each end of the tray's lip. With the rim of the tray resting on a 2-by-4 or other firm wooden surface, make a small indentation in the metal at each hole location, using the hammer and center punch or nail. With a drill bit that matches the diameter of the screws, and using the indentations as guides, drill your two holes, again making

A Tool-Caddy Towel Rack is put to use in the garden shed. A collection of garden nozzles makes a stronger statement grouped together than they would if scattered around the shed.

sure to work on top of a wooden drill-safe surface. Wear safety goggles while drilling.

2. Once you've drilled the holes in the shelf, use a pencil to mark the related hole positions on the wall. Use a level to ensure that the shelf will be straight. Insert the wall anchors into the wall.

3. As you attach the shelf to the wall, use a washer between the screw head and the shelf face for a sturdier and tighter fit.

(Left) The trio of a Tool-Caddy Towel Rack, Golf-Club Trellis, and mailbox planter lets the visitor know that a salvage gardener lives here. (Right) Insert a ball of twine into the cavity of a ceramic teapot, pull the twine end out the spout, tie a pair of scissors onto the handle, and it's at the ready to tie up droopy plants.

Auger or Spindle Paper-Towel Holder

Combining metal odds and ends to form a new creation is one of the signatures of the Salvage Studio. This paper-towel holder was one of our first creations. The bottom of a domed cheese server makes a good base. Augers can be found at many garage or estate sales that have old tools available, and spindles can be taken from broken dining or rocking chairs.

Materials:

- Finished wooden circle (painted or stained), approximately 9 to 10 inches in diameter
- Auger bit or wooden spindle, approximately 14 inches long, with a diameter small enough to fit a paper towel roll over
- 5-pound circular metal weight from a weight-lifting set, with a hole in the center wide enough for the auger to fit through
- Wooden drawer knob (optional)

Tools:

- Ruler
- Pencil
- Center punch
- Hammer
- Hand-held power drill or drill press
- Drill bit slightly smaller in diameter than your auger or spindle diameter
- Safety goggles
- Round wood file
- Rubber mallet
- Small piece of scrap wood (optional)

1. Find the center of the wooden circle by turning it upside down and drawing a straight line across the diameter in one direction. Rotate the circle and repeat this process. The point where they intersect is the center. Use a center punch and hammer to make a dimple in the wooden circle before drilling. It will keep the drill bit from skipping.
2. Wearing safety goggles, drill a hole in the wooden circle. It should be slightly smaller than the diameter of the auger or spindle.
3. Use the round wood file to gradually enlarge the hole so that the auger or spindle will fit very snugly.

Castoff items combine to make a salvage-style paper-towel holder. It's a great use for the abundance of metal weights found at yard sales.

4. When the hole is the right dimension, place the metal weight over the hole and insert the auger (with the point up) or spindle.

5. Tap the auger or spindle with a rubber mallet to ensure that it is in the hole securely. If you are using an auger as your upright piece, place a small piece of scrap wood over the point before you hit it with the mallet. Then screw the wooden drawer knob onto the auger point to protect yourself and your loved ones.

6. Place a paper towel roll over the auger or spindle for a one-of-a-kind paper-towel holder.

organize

Organization truly does make life easier, and there are so many varied and fun ways to be organized that it doesn't need to feel like a drag. I think most of us are pleased, if not downright delighted, when we think of something we'd like to use and can find it on the first try. Who wants to waste time looking here and there for something? As a full-time collector of stuff, I find this especially challenging; I needed to come up with ways to track all the stuff I am constantly amassing.

———

A popular feature at our studio is our shelves of cans and various metal containers which hold ephemera for sale and also are used during our workshops. Bottle-cap magnets make functional and eye-pleasing price markers.

The first thing to do is create a designated spot in your home for incoming stuff to land. Your keys, cell phone, and mail, plus odds and ends, always get put in this spot. It's where your outside life merges with your inside life. View it also as a filtering station.

I love the mail. Even in this technical age, I still regularly receive handmade cards, an item from an art mail swap, and magazines with pretty pictures. I save these things for dessert, though, and open the important but boring mail first. Junk mail gets a quick scan to see if any of it can be used for future art projects. At the Salvage Studio, we have a group that meets monthly to exchange artist trading cards. We decide on a theme every other month, one of which was to use junk mail

We Love Message Boards!

The possibilities are endless for message boards made out of salvaged pieces. The base piece can be large or small, but try to avoid items that are heavy or difficult to hang. Most require magnets—another source of boundless creativity (see "Magnet Test")—but here are some of our favorites:

Pot lids: Group together three of various sizes.

Old tools: Look for ones with flattened surfaces, such as scrapers or mortar/mastic spreaders.

Graters: Use one large, flat grater, or group a few small ones.

Stovetop toasters: Old-fashioned round toasters that fit over burners have wires that are ready-made for holding messages.

Film canister lids: What else can you do with these after converting 126 yards of 35mm film to DVD?

Baking sheets: These are especially appropriate for kitchen placement.

Silver-plated or metal floral-painted serving trays: For an elegant reminder to take out the trash!

Odd metal doors or shallow drawers: Remove the drawers from old file cabinets or metal boxes.

to create artistic cards. The results were a hoot! Paper that is not art-worthy is quickly placed in the recycling bin. Done. Bills or correspondence needing prompt attention require a home of their own. I've learned that it's dangerous to put these papers in a drawer or a file folder, because I tend to forget about them. Designate a vintage wire basket, metal dish rack, or silver-plated toast rack to hold these papers within easy view. Select something that isn't too large or you'll be back to digging. I receive very few catalogs these days, but I will confess that I do save some until the next one arrives. They live in a colorful school locker basket. As I add the latest catalog, I move the previous one to the recycling bin. It's a small victory.

Lisa and I have a group of friends we meet with once a month to practice new art techniques. We call them the artgirls. One of our artgirl friends recently asked everyone in our group what magazines they subscribe to. I realized that I receive at least 10 a month! Plus I am one of those people you see at the library and the bookstore, sitting and skimming through more magazines. The current unread ones at my home have a basket of their own. After I read them, some get passed around. Some are hoarded for a while. But eventually, I tear out favorite articles, pictures, or ideas and save them into a nifty filing system. I've made folders for garden, home, travel, holiday, gift, and my particular interests. They are little acts of optimism. I might not ever travel to a particular country, but if the opportunity arose, boy, would I be prepared! The folders are held in a rescued rusty brass record holder. The top level, which previously held the 45s, holds the files, and the lower level holds folders of crafting papers, organized by color. The record holder sits in my art studio where it offers easy access, looks interesting, and even has wheels for mobility (see the Record-Holder Organizer project). It could just as easily hold your car records, insurance papers, receipts, and more.

Off the Wall

Look at your walls for the next frontier of organizing. We love baby-crib springs. Baby cribs in general are easy to come by, and all their parts have uses. But the springs, in particular, are a convenient size and flat, so they easily attach to a wall space over your desk for a quick and varied organizer (see the Bedsprings Wall Organizer project). If you are a crafter and have oodles of ribbon, you can hang rows of ribbon spools from the top part of your spring organizer. Pull off as much ribbon as you need for a project and admire it the rest of the time.

Hammer a simple hole through the edge of a plain tin can, add a split ring from the office supply store or an old keychain, and hang it wherever you wish on the springs for accessible storage. Set up rows of cans or arrange them artistically. No commitment necessary—you can change your mind and the cans' configuration.

Corral your household ball of string or twine in a large old funnel. Attach it to the springs in the same way you attached the cans, and feed the end of the string out of the small end of the funnel. A metal conical sieve used for making jelly is another ideal twine holder. Bend the handle upward so it will lie flat on the wall, and add a small hole in the bottom of the sieve for the twine to feed outward. Make two, one for your crib springs organizer and one to keep outside, near your potting bench, with a small pair of scissors tied to it.

A small message board created from a dustpan or other unusual metal piece can hold business cards and add to the appeal of your hardworking wall organizer. Or you can use simple clothespins clipped to the springs

---

Old wood checkers glued to magnets corral a few papers on a 35mm film canister lid.

to attach notes to yourself, invitations to upcoming events, and take-out menus.

Use old window shutters to hold ideas, cards, or photos. The shutters can hang vertically or horizontally on the wall. Simply knot a pretty ribbon to the hinges of the shutter to hang them horizontally. If you have three taller shutters, you can hinge them together to create a freestanding organizer. This piece could do double duty as a small screen in a room to hide something less than scenic and hold your family photos at the same time.

Another wall-worthy idea is the bicycle-wheel organizer. Two essential components of this are a spare wheel and a piece of wood to mount it on, such as an orphaned cupboard door. Both are easily found on the junking circuit. Pieced together with a screw, washer, and nut, your wheel will even spin after it is mounted! (See the Bicycle-Wheel Organizer project.) At the Boeing Surplus Store (a veritable Disneyland for junkers

---

Magnet Test

Keep a magnet handy whenever you head out to garage sales or other salvage sites, to test your metal pieces for magnet ability. They are also a good way to tell whether or not your metal is ferrous (contains iron).

And speaking of magnets, at the Salvage Studio we make them from a variety of knick-knacks (using our favorite heavy-duty glue for interior use—E6000). Some of our most common magnetic creations include:

- Bottle caps
- Dominoes, checkers, Scrabble letters, dice, or other game pieces
- Candle clips once used for Christmas trees
- Large washers with oddball metal nuts and pieces glued together
- Clip earrings and small brooches with the backs removed
- Tiny tart baking pans
- Foreign coins
- Buttons

---

like us that is, sadly, closing, but look for a similar manufacturer's surplus store near you), we found a bin of giant circular saw blade holders made from wood. Lisa designed her own wheel of fortune for garden chores, using sections of a picket fence and Scrabble letters that spelled out "weed," "water," "prune," "plant," and "rest." Or your wheel organizer could live near your gardening supplies and hold seeds or your gardening gloves, with the help of some clothespins.

One Step at a Time

What's so valuable about these salvage projects is that they allow you to tackle one small portion of your life at a time. If you are just starting to get your home organized, you can start small. And if it's a task you are not looking forward to, try Lisa's technique: Tell yourself you are going to do "it" (organize your desk, file your recipes, straighten the potting bench) for just 15 minutes. Oftentimes, once you have started you forget about the clock.

Another simple tip for organizing is to go around your home and garage and corral all of the things you need for one purpose in one spot. Think "like with like." For example, gather all your stamps, letter-writing supplies, any birthday and occasion cards, address book, and calendar. I keep track of birthdays in a simple little book organized by month. It's a permanent record that is easily updated. At the beginning of each month, I check my book and address and stamp cards to everyone having a birthday that month. The really hard part for me is then remembering to send the cards a few days

---

Divide and conquer your small crafting items with lovely canning jars. Put only one kind of item in each jar for easy retrieval; besides being so useful, the jars offer a visual unity.

ahead. Store this list of birthdays with your stationery supplies in a wood or metal tool caddy. Tool caddies vary in size. A smaller one could tuck inside a cupboard, but visibility is our friend, so don't tuck it too deep.

My biggest challenge is keeping my head above water with the influx of raw materials and creative fodder that accumulates in our garage. With the goal of someday parking one of my family's cars in the three-car garage, with each trip out there, I try to bring one thing inside the house, make a decision about it, and find a home for it. And I've made a rule for myself, which I usually follow, of washing things *before* they get put in the garage. I've learned the hard way about bringing unwanted insects inside, and so I budget time after hitting an estate sale for a period of cleaning. Small items that I can't wash, such as books, old textiles, pillows, and such, I wrap in plastic and place in the freezer for three days or up to a week. This will kill any larvae of future generations of critters. Your family or housemates might have a bit of an adventure looking for the ice cream, but I doubt that a pillow or two will hamper their search. As I evolve into a wiser junker, I try hard to not let stuff land in the garage in the first place. I swear that it glues itself to that concrete floor within minutes.

You can get yourself organized over time, but what is really tricky is staying organized. Wall organizers keep your stuff highly visible. I've learned that I have to see things. Clear containers work, of course, but the ubiquitous plastic boxes have so little soul. Balance them out with our rescued relic ideas. A well-used metal lunchbox can hold letters that need answering on your desk. A muffin tin can separate your clips, pushpins, and rubber bands. Rolls of wrapping paper are easily stored and accessed in a metal wire shopping cart. The papers are pretty and look festive side by side in the handy container. If they slip through the cart's bottom wire grid, simply cut out a piece of cardboard to fit inside the bottom. (This container gets extra convenience points because it also has wheels. Casters and wheels on any container are helpful.) If your container is not open or transparent, label like crazy. You want your system to be user friendly for whomever you might share your home with.

———

This perfect piece of red metal was found in an outbuilding during our Oregon farm adventure. S hooks are instant hangers for the mesh portion, and magnets could hold an array of notes on the bottom section.

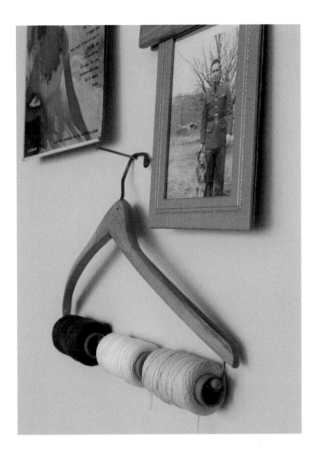

After a strategic snip of a metal part of the hanger, a handy twine holder is born. Place your favorite colors of the moment on it, and you are ready to roll.

———

Another basic strategy for staying organized is to make sure there's room to add more. I am sometimes just one great free pile or church rummage sale away from the system not working! For example, perhaps you collect bottle caps and want to keep them all in one location. If you've chosen a container that is too small, what do you do once it is full? It's much too easy to start a second location, and spreading things around defeats the purpose of organizing collections and materials. Choose a roomy enough container or—gasp—stop

acquiring that item. Currently I'm enjoying the look of my stored crafting ephemera—keys, crystals, dominoes, wooden bingo markers, wooden game letters, and broken jewelry bits are all gathered in large old canning jars and giant glass food containers. The clear jars remind me to use their contents, but the larger assembly also creates an artistic, textured display.

No More Tangles

I love jewelry. I love handmade jewelry. And I love to admire my pieces and see them displayed. As a result, I'm always on the lookout for fireplace tool holders. With so many homes using gas fireplaces these days, you

More Cleaning Action

We try to stick to an organic approach to cleaning whenever possible. But I often want faster results and less wear and tear on my wrists, given the hours of cleaning our work requires. Here are a few tried-and-true methods:

A paste of **baking soda** with a small amount of water makes a gentle all-purpose scrub.

Lisa swears by **toothpaste** for polishing silver.

Stubborn sticky substances, like old price sticker residue, are best removed with **citrus-based cleaners** such as Goo Gone. I've dutifully tried peanut butter and canola oil without much satisfaction.

When in doubt, spray something with white vinegar—a natural and safe disinfectant.

can easily find sets of fireplace tools. The holders are typically metal and often gorgeous sculptured shapes. Most holders are in a U shape, which is perfect for hanging necklaces and bracelets, while the little tray on the bottom is good for pins and other pieces.

Don't chuck the tools, however. The pokers make sturdy hose guards to protect your garden beds from wild watering hoses. Lisa searches for tools that look like letters of the alphabet to use in her junk word signs. Amy collects the handles of fireplace tools because they usually screw off and feature threaded holes, which have a variety of uses. She once found a beautiful magnifying glass at a yard sale that had no handle; she was able to attach it to a fireplace tool handle. A handle can also act as a curtain rod end or as a fine finial for a decorative piece.

Another idea for organizing jewelry is to stack silver plate into a pedestal formation (see the Serving Pedestals project in the Entertain chapter). My pedestal holds favorite flower pins made from recycled, felted (shrunken) wool sweaters and retro fabrics. And if you run across a dressmaker's form, snap it up. The wire mesh one in Amy's house is a work of art; they can be put to work holding your favorite jewelry pieces, among other possibilities.

At the Salvage Studio, we sell hundreds of ephemera and have most of them organized in tin cans with a bottle-cap-magnet price affixed to the can. What could look like an utter mess instead looks orderly and is easy for us to maintain. One of our business neighbors, Romio's Pizza, saves their large No.10 size cans for us, which hold the larger items. We've become can connoisseurs! And customers cannot resist taking a peek inside each one.

(Above) A wonderful dress form holds a handmade pin fashioned from gathered circles of ribbon, velvet leaves, and an eye-catching celluloid button. Brighten up your lapel, purse, hat, or lampshade with this beauty. (Right) Which came first—storage or display? This combination showcases jewelry as art, while so much else can be socked away in those drawers and suitcases and still be accessible.

When possible, use your collections themselves for storage and staying organized. A long time ago, I started to collect both wooden and tin picnic baskets. It didn't take me long to figure out that this collection was taking up lots of room. The baskets stacked on top of each other, which helped. I then filled them with items we don't use very often—winter hats in one, gloves in another, and such. One was even dedicated to being our actual picnic basket, ready to go with everything we needed but the food. Amy collects vintage suitcases and has them stacked in a very tall and visually stunning display in her hallway. Inside, she stashes linens for the guest bedroom, which is right around the corner, extra

quilts, decor pillows, throws, and her display items that are not being used.

When it comes to managing errands, we've all learned that a little bit of planning saves time, money, and gas. I am a list maker. (It's such a relief to get a thought out of my too-full brain and saved on a piece of paper!) So I created a keychain that can hold my errand list by fastening a small alligator clip to a rummage-sale antique key fob. Your existing keychain, a handmade creation from beads, an old medal—anything will do as the keychain base. I leave my keychain, with my paper note attached, dangling out of my purse, so with any luck, when I look at my purse, I'll remember I need to stop by the grocery store, pick up cat food, or leave a few minutes early to get gas.

Be nice to yourself—with each piece of paper filed or recycled, each item stowed in the garage, or each remembered errand, don't think about how much is left to do; instead, appreciate how much you have accomplished so far.

———

A Paris flea market keychain with a small clip attached holds last-minute reminder notes.

Record-Holder Organizer

Store the files you use most often in this handy record holder for instant accessibility. Or use it to hold books, magazines, or even plates. It's great in your office or at your next buffet. The hardest part of this project will be finding a vintage record holder, which really isn't that hard. The ones we find most often are made of thick, brass-colored wire with a row of slots on top for the old 45s and the bottom row designed to hold LP/33rpm records. My favorite models have wheels, which makes your file holder more versatile and convenient.

Materials:
- Record holder

Tools:
- Heavy-duty wire cutters
- Metal file

1. Usually the slats in the top row of the record holder are too close together to hold a file folder. Take your

Files and function on wheels are combined with this converted record holder. A magnet message board and a ribbon holder frame complete the organized picture.

wire cutters and snip out every other metal piece.

2. If a little sharp nub of metal remains, take a metal file and smooth it down. If you plan to store fatter files in the top row, snip out more metal dividers.

Bedsprings Wall Organizer

This versatile piece could be put to work in your office, kitchen, or garage. Finding a vintage baby crib is a bit of a challenge because they do not show up at the thrift stores due to safety regulations. Newer styles are easiest to find. Put the word out among your friends and family to see if they have an unused crib they would like to donate to the cause.

Materials:

- Baby crib
- Tin cans of various sizes
- Split rings at least 1 inch in diameter
- 4 yards sturdy, decorative ribbon (enough for 3 rows across to run through ribbon spools)
- Medium to large funnel
- Ball of string
- Metal dustpan with several magnets
- Wooden clothespins

The springs from the bottom of a baby crib offer a strong graphic look for any wall, and can hold as much or as little as you like.

Tools:

- Screwdrivers—flat and Phillips head—for dismantling
- Discarded phone book or wooden or nylon cutting board used for projects
- Awl
- Hammer
- Metal file
- Pinking shears or fabric scissors

Baby Crib Redux!

The two longer sides of a baby crib frame can be easily converted to hold paper, magazines, or towels (see the Wooden-Crib Rack project). Its flexible side ribbon supports allow it to be freestanding or closed flat and propped against a wall.

The head and foot boards of the crib (if they are solid) make terrific chalkboards. A few coats of blackboard paint give you two charming message boards.

1. The springs are usually easily lifted out of the crib. On some models, you may need to remove a few screws to remove the spring component.

2. To prepare your cans for hanging, place them on their side on a section of old phone book or a wooden or plastic cutting board reserved for projects. Use the awl and hammer to punch a small hole near the open top edge of the can, hammering against the flat surface. The outside edge of your hole will be rough, so use a metal file to smooth the edges.

3. Attach a split ring to a can and then to the springs. A row of cans across the bottom is usually very handy. A larger No.10 (restaurant-size) can will hold bulky things, and 28-ounce cans are a great size for most other items.

4. To attach rows of ribbon for holding spools of ribbon or hanging special cards, photos, or invitations, cut lengths of sturdy ribbon (grosgrain is a good choice) the width of the springs plus 2 more feet. Attach the ribbon to a split ring with a knot, leaving a tail of 6 inches or so on both ends. Trim your ribbon ends with pinking shears or at a slant or in a V-shaped wedge cut into the edge with fabric scissors.

5. You can attach a funnel to hold a ball of string in the same way you attached the tin can.

6. A small message board created from a metal dustpan can be hung in an open area.

7. Wooden clothespins attached here and there are useful for holding single paper items.

Wooden-Crib Rack

Hang sheets of wrapping paper in your craft area, towels in your bathroom, or magazines next to your favorite reading chair.

Materials:
- Baby crib
- 3½ to 4 yards sturdy, decorative ribbon

Tools:
- Screwdrivers—flat and Phillips head—for dismantling
- Center punch
- Hammer
- Cordless drill
- ¼- and ⅜-inch drill bits
- Safety goggles
- Pinking shears or fabric scissors

1. Detach the wooden sides from the crib with a screwdriver. A few pieces of metal hardware will remain on the crib sides; remove them as well.

2. Arrange the sides into an inverted V shape. Some

pieces may have the perfect hole waiting for you to slip your sturdy ribbon through for tying. Usually, however, you have to drill a couple of matching holes in one or both pieces, 1 inch from the top where the two sides will connect. Create a pilot hole with a center punch and hammer, and start drilling with a ¼-inch drill bit. Wear safety goggles while drilling. Increase the size of the hole with the larger ⅜-inch drill bit. You want a hole big enough to thread your piece of ribbon through, but not so big that it splits the wood.

3. Cut two pieces of ribbon, each 24 inches long. Thread one piece through the holes on one side, fastening it with a knot. Trim the ends decoratively. Repeat on the other side.

4. Cut two more pieces of ribbon, each 36 inches long. Place each ribbon on opposite sides about halfway down the height of the crib sides, to prevent the crib sides from opening too far. Loop each ribbon piece through the farthest outside slat of the two rail pieces on one side and make a knot, creating a hinge about 10 inches long. Repeat on the other side. Trim the edges to match the others.

Only one side of the wooden crib rack is in use in this picture to conserve valuable floor space. But in an instant, it can be converted into the two-sided version by spreading apart the bottom sections.

Bicycle-Wheel Organizer

Exercise your wall space for to-do lists, invitations, bills to pay, garden chores, or your extra packages of seeds. The wooden backing for this project should be slightly larger than the circumference of your wheel and thick enough to support the weight of the wheel after it is attached. A cupboard door is ideal because as a rule they are nice and thick and are often outlined in wooden molding for a framed, finished look.

Materials:
- Lone wheel from any size or model of bike
- Sturdy piece of wood, approximately ¾-inch thick and large enough to leave a 1- to 2-inch border around the wheel
- Metal screw, ¼ inch in diameter and 4 inches long, with a washer and nut
- 2 sturdy wood screws, each ½-inch long
- 18-gauge wire for hanger

Tools:
- Pencil
- Multipurpose rotary tool (if necessary)
- Hand-held power drill
- ¼-inch drill bit
- Safety goggles
- Center punch
- Hammer

1. The wheel will probably need a good scrubbing to remove grease and grime. You can remove the tire and tube or leave them if they're in fine condition and you like the look of it.
2. Center your wheel in the middle of your wood and mark the center of the axle hole on your wood with a pencil.
3. Select a metal screw with a head large enough to not slip through the axle hole of the wheel. Choose one long enough to go through the wheel and wood with approximately ½-inch extra in the back of the wood for a nut and washer. If the screw is longer than necessary, cut off the extra length, using the cut-off wheel on a multipurpose rotary tool. (Wear safety goggles when cutting and drilling.)
4. Drill a hole in the wood where you marked it. It should be large enough to let your metal screw pass through.
5. Slip the screw through the bicycle wheel and the hole and attach a washer and nut on the back side of the wood.

6. To create a hanger, use a center punch and hammer to create two pilot holes, each at a point approximately 4 inches from the side of the wood and 4 inches from the top.

Wooden clothespins work well to secure items to the spokes because this wheel can still spin. It will cheer you up to give your chores a whirl or two.

7. Attach a wood screw in each spot, leaving a small gap between the head of the screw and the board.

8. Wrap a length of sturdy wire between the two screws, securing the ends under and around the screw heads and creating a slight arch in the wire, about 1 inch high. Use an extra-strong wall hanger, such as one suggested for mirrors, to hang this heavy piece.

LISA

look

At the Salvage Studio, we tend to look at things a little differently. That's one reason people enjoy visiting us. They want to see how we use various found items and reinvent them. But we believe anyone can reimagine these things. We just have more practice.

Remember as a child lying in the grass and finding animals and shapes in the clouds? Looking at everyday things in a new way, you can recapture that same imagination process but add a practical twist. Soon you will be seeing alternate uses for everything.

Turn Things Upside Down

One of our favorite things to do at the Studio is turn something upside down to see what it might become in its next life. As a matter of fact, many times we look at things upside down in the first place because we don't really know what they are or what their original purpose

was. It's an easy way to reinvent an item and to explore its potential as an interesting and unusual object in its own right.

We were called recently to pick up some items from a lovely older woman named Marie. She had grown up on a farm and had held on to some of the farm's implements and was now willing to share them with us. One of our favorites was a rusted heavy-duty pulley from a barn, probably used for moving hay bales. When we flipped it over, the pulley became the base of a pedestal, with a round hole that a bowl or tray would fit into. Beth found the perfect-size silver-plated bowl, and presto! We had a one-of-a-kind buffet server. We love

With a simple hanging lamp socket from a hardware store, a wire mesh trash can is now an attractive lampshade that maximizes the light over an elegant table setting.

please help yourself

Our Top 10 Tools

Lineman's pliers. These have a larger "nose" than needle-nose pliers, providing more area to grab, hold, and grip. They are great for pulling stubborn nails out of wood or closing up an S hook.

Sewing seam gauge. This small sewing tool is perfect for measuring in small increments. With the adjustable slide, you can accurately measure distances without a second thought—was that $1\frac{3}{8}$ or $1\frac{7}{8}$?

Small ball-peen hammer. The smaller shape and heft are ideal when working in tight spots, such as when flattening brass brads on paper projects. The small, rounded head also provides an easy way to give that "hammered" look to metal projects.

Multipurpose rotary tools such as the Dremel are wonderful creatures. They pack the wallop of the bigger tools (electric drill, power sander) but are so much easier to use, and their small size makes them ideal for small hands. The metal cutting disc is especially handy. This attachment makes short work of trimming screws that are too long, removing rusty links, or disassembling any metal piece for reconstruction into a new project.

Rubber mallet. Useful for encouraging objects to go the direction you want without leaving dent marks.

Phone books. Most can be divided into several sections to make very functional work surfaces for drilling and pounding.

Round-nose pliers are good for bending wire into beautiful loops and swoops without marring the wire or leaving irregular, harsh edges.

Metal hand punch. Our favorite one resembles a heavy-duty paper punch and comes with seven punch sizes from Harbor Freight Tools (a national chain). Costing less than $20, this tool is easy to use and punches through heavy pieces of metal, leaving a clean hole. We fondly refer to ours as "Big Earl."

Good scissors. This is the pair you hide from your friends and family members. You don't want anyone cutting duct tape with these! Buying good scissors is like buying knives for the kitchen—any knife will cut most things, but your favorite cuts everything. Have a separate pair for fabric and ribbon that is not used for paper. Cutting paper dulls the blade, and dull scissors will fray fabric and ribbon ends when you cut them.

Cordless drill. Spend a little extra to get one with decent power and an extra battery pack. Don't wait until you're in your 50s (like Beth) to discover power tools!

Create a warm glow indoors or out: Place metal box graters over glass votive holders for instant luminaries along a walkway, or cluster three together on a silver-plated tray to brighten a holiday display.

the contrast of rust and silver plate. Don't be afraid to mix metal, glass, and silver-plated surfaces. It creates an exciting juxtaposition of elements that keeps people on their toes.

Amy was looking for an unusual lampshade for her

Try Something New

Sometimes we need permission to be brave and try something new. We love our multipurpose rotary tools and use them in workshops. We find that most people own one but don't use it very often, and some have never used it. We encourage them to give it a try in a safe and supervised environment. We have the safety goggles out, the protected surface ready to go, and all the encouragement and support they need. We have a specific project and item that needs to be drilled, sanded, or cut. By limiting the choices, we can hopefully bypass the overwhelmed feeling that usually kicks in when someone mentions power tools. We demo the technique that works for us and then let them try. It is very rewarding to see the confidence in their faces when they drill through a Scrabble tile for the first time or learn how to change the bits.

dining room and chanced upon a wire wastepaper basket matching the shape and size she needed. She made a hole in the bottom, flipped it over, and threaded a hanging lamp socket through the hole. Her new lamp hangs over the dining room table, where it creates a graphic, modern look while providing maximum light.

Create a garden surprise using a trio of upside-down golf clubs to form a nearly instant garden trellis. Pick clubs in colors that accent your plantings or add a punch of color to a bloomed-out area (see the Golf-Club Trellis project). And rest assured, these clubs won't cause divots in your lawn.

Turning objects upside down is a quick way to gain a new perspective and look at things in a unique way.

Uncommon Uses for Common Objects

We try not to let an item's original use hold us back. It is a personal challenge to find a new and improved use for everything. A typical decorating dilemma is how to display artwork. An uncommon solution is men's pants hangers. They have a built-in hanging device—a soft clamping mechanism—and are readily available. Insert a vintage record cover, a family photograph, or a favorite poster where you would normally place the pants, clamp down, and hang for instant impact. Arrange in a group of three or five and select your art by color or theme. You can change your selections with the seasons or when the mood strikes without having to get out a hammer. This is an especially good technique for displaying your child's art project of the week or favorite softcover books. Kids can change their own artwork whenever they wish, and it will limit the number of holes in the walls.

A classic metal mop bucket spends its life holding water. Next time, fill it with frozen water in the form of crushed ice and use it as an ice chest or beverage holder for an outdoor event. Many older buckets have wheels and can move around with the party. An old wheelbarrow is also a good mobile ice chest. When the festivities are over and the ice is melted, just wheel it to a dry garden spot and recycle the water into the garden.

Curious cats, wagging dogs, and running children

Join together a silver-plated wine goblet and a glass dish with a spot of glue. Add a candle to grace your table, or give as a gift to brighten someone's day.

can all wreak havoc on our decor. A simple and elegant solution for displaying your tiniest items is to place them on a silver-plated tray and then cover them with a classic clear glass cheese dome as a cloche. It creates a sense of importance for your treasured objects and gives them a place of honor. It also keeps hard-to-dust items clean, protected, and away from paws and little fingers. Add a fancy ribbon around the handle to complement your decor. Keep the wooden or marble base of the cheese dome to use in another project, like the Auger or Spindle Paper-Towel Holder described in the Begin chapter. You never know when you will need a nicely finished round piece of wood.

Remember making luminaries out of tin cans? You would nail out your design on the side of the can, place a candle inside, and watch the pattern come alive. But in your kitchen is an instant luminary: a box cheese grater. It is already poked full of holes and stands straight and tall. Place a tea light on a saucer, place your grater over the lit candle, and enjoy the show. For impact, group three graters together on a tray for a lovely centerpiece. Of course, you will probably want to grate cheese at some point, so comb garage sales and thrift stores for older graters to use as luminaries and keep your good one for cheese.

We love the graphic combination of black, white, and silver, so we often use dominoes as decorating accents. Placed in a glass jar or arranged on a silver-plated tray, they provide a fun diversion on the coffee

Drawers—they're not just for socks anymore! Lightly sand a chipped, peeling wooden drawer, add a fun knob, and hang on the wall for a decorative shelf. Group several together for a great display.

table when entertaining or while talking on the phone. Glue them to a silver-plated tray to create a stunning clock that is both beautiful and functional (see the Domino Clock project). The juxtaposition of the silver plate with the game pieces makes it suitable for a formal dining area or a family room.

Silver-plated utensils have many uncommonly clever uses. Use odds and ends of silverware to make new handles for your kitchen cabinets, hooks for your bath towels, or easels for small cards, photos, or place-card holders for a dinner party (see the Silverware Handles and Pulls and the Fork Easels projects). You can also decorate yourself by making a necklace pendant from an old fork. The bent tines are the perfect place to hang a selection of favorite charms (see the Fork Pendant Necklace project).

Fresh Eyes, Fresh Spaces

When my husband, Doug, and I first moved into our house, we had a mishmash of furniture. (Come to think of it, I guess we still do.) My friend Susan asked if she could move furniture around for me. Because she has an excellent sense of design—her house always looks divine—and I consider her a role model for creative thinking, I jumped at the offer. She started by moving everything out to our covered carport. Then she opened the garage doors and began moving in odds and ends of furniture I was storing that I didn't know what to do with. She would place things one at a time and see how they worked, all the while creating cozy seating arrangements and a reading nest for me. She asked a lot of questions, like, "When you walk in the door, where do you put your stuff?" "Why do you keep your magazines there?" "Does this tchotchke have meaning for you?"

I learned that having someone look at my belongings with more objectivity can bring out qualities in them that I hadn't recognized. Someone else can see uses for your items that you never dreamed possible. After Susan's input, I now store my kitchen linens in my grandfather's drop-front desk, which is far more

Two Think Green creations. Both artists received the same can of items: One created a minimalist Seattle skyline; the other, a musical marvel complete with chimes, drum, and shaker.

interesting and appropriate for my small house than a big buffet. Plus, it has sentimental meaning for me. What I also appreciated about this process was that we didn't need to run out and buy new things to get a whole new look. Most of us already have more than enough stuff. And when you do eventually find or buy items to add to the mix, you'll have a clearer vision of what you need and what will work. This saves time, money, and waste.

Another friend, Cindy, was in a decorating rut of her own and asked a group of her artsy friends to come over and redecorate her home. She let them have free rein because she trusted their design aesthetic and loved how they had decorated their own homes. She prepared for the new look by removing everything from the walls and gathering up all those items that she felt could be used in the new decor. Each friend picked a room and started trying out different combinations on the walls. Cindy ultimately tweaked a few things, but all in all, the friends created spaces she loved.

At the Salvage Studio, we recently helped our friend Colleen restyle her front garden space. Colleen had added some newly salvaged garden furniture and rusty metal pieces to an already large collection of interesting items. Her outdoor area had become overwhelming, and she needed some help with editing. When we live with items for a while, we get used to seeing them how and wherever they are placed. It takes fresh eyes to see what's not working or what might be a better use. This "fresh eyes" approach can work for indoor or outdoor spaces, furniture placement, or just rehanging pictures on a wall. Once you get started sharing ideas, even more fun will develop—as well as happy memories of time with friends.

Think Green

At the Studio, March is always Think Green month. To commemorate this theme, each year we hold a creative event: We put together 50 large cans of found objects and interesting materials, keeping the contents of each can identical. There is a good mixture of metal, glass, fabric, and wood items. Artists purchase cans for a small donation to the Re-Store (a local construction salvage nonprofit company in Seattle), and then they are challenged to come up with a work of art using everything in the can, as well as the can itself. They can add components if they wish, but they have to use everything they receive from us. At the unveiling of the creations (on St. Patrick's Day—a wee bit of green!), we are impressed by the salvaged art that results. We've had a Seattle skyline "painting," a bird feeder, a working musical instrument, and folk-art animals and flowers—all designed from our cans of junk.

The energy this activity creates is phenomenal. The cans fly out the door, and as the completed objects are returned, we hear stories of the creative process. Inevitably, it results in someone finally cleaning out their craft space or garage in order to work on the project. One person at last laid to rest some past issue with an art instructor who said something to suppress her creativity in childhood. Others made their art piece in memory of a loved one or to commemorate a special occasion in their life. The stories are as beautiful as the works of art.

We display the finished pieces for the month of March. It is quite a sight to see all the creations together and to see how a group of people can all have the same items and see different things in them.

Sharing Solutions, Building Community

For many of us, the solutions to our everyday clutter are in our own backyards or neighborhoods. The fact is that most people want to find good homes for their unwanted objects. At the Studio, we provide an interesting solution by reinventing something and finding it a new home. It's exciting for former owners to know that their stuff is getting a new life. Many times we hook up two people on the spot—one wants broken china for a mosaic project, the other has a box full of broken china perfect for mosaics—and hope they connect on some other level or find out they are neighbors. We also love being able to share the story of how an object came to us. That way people's stories, their lives, and the things they loved and collected aren't forgotten.

We were lucky enough to salvage the basement of Elmer, a metal worker with a penchant for collecting odds and ends. At some point in his life he manufactured a bunch of minimailboxes of sheet metal for a craft project. Many were not completed, but we loved them anyway. We knew they had potential as pencil holders, flower vases, and who knows what else. And we get to tell the new owners that Elmer made them.

The saying that "Many hands make light work" holds

true at the Salvage Studio, where each of us contributes in different ways. Amy is our studio stylist and can visualize how individual objects we rescue and create fit into a larger setting. Beth is our marketing guru and hostess; she loves to make people feel welcome and special. I enjoy the practical, business side of the operation. Because each of us performs the duties we love and are good at, each of us is free to excel. We are all pieces of a puzzle, placed together in the right combination. This puzzle-piece picture can work for you too: look at your life and surround yourself with people who complement and augment your strengths.

In the process of writing this book, we realized that no one person can be good at all these things: enter

taining, gardening, decorating, organizing, saving the world. (Even Martha has a staff of hundreds!) So we split up the chapters to reflect our different talents. It works as a whole because of our shared love of salvage, recycling, and crafts.

We have also found that people need to plan fun. And it is much more fun to play with friends. By planning adult playtime, either through workshops or play dates, and having convenient access to a work space and supplies, you give your mind the freedom to create. And most of the time the sum of the parts of a group is far greater than the individuals themselves. Watching someone else create helps and inspires some people. Many times we just don't know where to begin, and even if the style isn't ours, sharing the process can free the mind and spark our own ideas. During workshops we provide just a few token examples of the finished project, because at the end of the two hours our attendees typically have created superior works of art. The group dynamic is very powerful; you encourage one another and it just builds from there!

Our modern lifestyles can contribute to an isolated feeling. We spend the weekdays at work in our office. Evenings and weekends are often spent at home, usually with family or doing household chores. This makes it difficult to connect with people. Creating art also tends to be a solitary activity, and that exacerbates the feelings of isolation. It's easy to get into a creating rut when we don't get feedback on our creations. Our internal editor can also be very critical, and that stifles our creativity too. But it's difficult to listen to that inner critic when

---

Travel the world without leaving your living room. Homage to France can be wishful thinking or pleasant memories.

Once a Day

Challenge yourself to find a new use for at least one thing each day:

Turn your object **upside down.** What do you see?

Discover an uncommon use for a common household item. Does a broom do anything besides sweep?

Ask a friend to consider your things from her unique perspective; agree to live with his or her changes for at least 24 hours!

Will your one thing **fit into** a larger work of art, a collection, or a display?

Think "green." Is there a **recycling alternative** to just tossing something?

---

surrounded by laughter and friends.

In the process of teaching at the Studio, I've found that we don't all interpret instructions in the same way—but that can be a good thing. By explaining and reexplaining a technique or project in different ways, I come up with more good ideas. In the act of reinterpreting a project or salvaged material for someone else, I myself see it from a new perspective.

Look to your community for salvage solutions, and create a community that will support you in your creative endeavors. You will be rewarded with new ideas, new confidence, and new friends.

Domino Clock

Keep time with this elegant clock made from dominoes. A silver-plated tray makes an excellent backdrop to the graphic dominoes. I like to use the double-number dominoes for the even hours. For example, a domino with four dots on each end represents eight o'clock.

Materials:

- Silver-plated tray, at least 12 inches in diameter
- 12 dominoes that denote the hours of the day
- Clock mechanism with clock hands that runs on batteries (available at hobby shops and craft stores)
- Heavy-duty adhesive, such as E6000

Tools:

- Pencil
- Ruler
- Center punch
- Hammer
- Hand-held power drill or drill press
- Drill bit (the clock kit will specify the size needed)
- Safety goggles
- Metal file

1. Find the center of the tray by turning it upside down and drawing a straight line across the diameter in one direction and then another. Where they intersect is the center.

2. Use a center punch and hammer to make a dimple in the center of the tray before drilling. It will keep the drill bit from skipping around.

3. Wearing safety goggles, drill a hole in the center of your silver-plated tray, using a hand-held drill or drill press. The diameter of the hole will be specified in the clock mechanism kit. You may need to file off any rough edges with a metal file. See "Drilling Silver Plate" for more information.

4. Arrange the dominoes around the tray. I start with the 12 and the 6, then the 3 and the 9, and then align the other numbers in between.

5. Glue the dominoes in place. Allow to dry for 24 hours.

6. Attach the clock mechanism to the tray, according to the package directions.

7. Set the time. You may need to adjust the hands by bending them upward slightly so they don't catch on each other as they rotate.

*The classic simplicity of the silver-plated tray and the
whimsy of the dominoes make this clock suitable for any room
in the home.*

Golf-Club Trellis

This trellis can be placed over a prized plant that needs a little support or in a container as an accent. Either wooden or metal clubs will do, depending on the look you want.

Materials:
- 3 golf clubs
- 1-foot length of 18-gauge copper wire

Tools:
- Needle-nose pliers

1. Hold the golf clubs in one hand, club ends up, with the three handles in a tripod shape on the ground.
2. Wrap wire tightly around the handles of all three clubs, at the base of the club heads. Copper wire is soft and easy to bend, but you may need a pair of needle-nose pliers to help you really twist the

wires tight at the end of the wrapping and to tuck in the ends.

(Left) A blue metal cart acts as a potting bench on wheels and holds Garden Goddesses, birdhouses, and gardener's essentials. (Right) Abandoned blue golf clubs are transformed into a Golf-Club Trellis to provide support for a young vine in a terra-cotta pot.

Fork Easels

This is a fun way to display a card or photos, and they also make elegant place-card holders. Forks with four tines, which are more stable, are recommended.

Materials:

- Silver-plated forks

Tools:

- Lineman's pliers
- Needle-nose pliers

1. Grab one of the outside tines of a fork with the lineman's pliers and bend it forward to about 90 degrees, flaring it out slightly. Hold most of the tine in the lineman's pliers for stability and even bending.
2. Repeat on the other side.
3. Bend the inside tines back to about 45 degrees.
4. Test the stability of the fork on a flat surface. The outside tines should rest evenly on a table, with the inside tines facing away from you. Make adjustments as needed.
5. Bend the tips of the outside tines upward with needle-nose pliers to make the holder part of the easel.

Fork Easels can hold place cards, be used to identify ingredients, or help greet guests.

ROQUEFORT

Silverware Handles and Pulls

In the Studio's kitchen, we installed silver-plated silverware as our cabinet handles and drawer pulls. It is one of our most asked-about projects. If you'll be using forks, we recommend installing them on upper cabinets so no one gets poked!

Materials:

- Assortment of silver-plated silverware
- Round-head machine screws with nuts, in various lengths
- Plastic spacers in assorted sizes, from ¼ inch to 1 inch long

Tools:

- Felt-tip pen
- Center punch
- Hammer
- Hand-held power drill or drill press
- Drill bits

Our kitchen cabinets at the Studio needed a face-lift, so we gave them one with a collage of dictionary pages coated with paste wax, a finishing touch that gives the pages an aged look and provides extra protection.

- Safety goggles
- Countersink bit (available at hardware stores) or small metal file
- Phillips head screwdriver

1. Figure out the placement of your pulls by holding the silverware up to the drawer or cabinet fronts. Good places to have your connections are the handles of knives, spoons, and forks and the bowls and blades of spoons and knives. Forks have a natural spot below the tines to place a screw through. Mark your chosen drill spots on the silverware with a felt-tip pen. You may have to fill some or all of the existing holes in the cabinet fronts and drawers with wood putty and repaint or refinish them. Then drill new holes to match the holes in the silverware handles.

2. Make a dimple in the silverware at each drilling spot with a center punch and hammer.

3. Wearing safety goggles, drill with a hand-held drill or drill press. Match the drill bit size to the size of the machine screws you have. See "Drilling Silver Plate" for more information.

4. Use a countersink bit or small file to smooth the rough edges around the holes on the silverware.

Drilling Silver Plate

When you want a clean-looking hole, it is time to reach for a drill. Getting the hang of power tools can be intimidating at first. Remind yourself that you have probably used a food processor or blender in the kitchen and have survived. A regular hand-held power drill will do the trick on many metals. If you plan to drill silver plate, especially cutlery, investing in a drill press is a good way to go.

Before drilling, use a hammer and a metal center punch or even a common nail to create small indentations in your metal pieces to serve as pilot holes. These indentations will keep your drill bit in place as you start to drill. Always wear safety goggles when drilling. Place a small section of plywood or any other extra wood piece, such as an old cutting board, underneath your metal piece. (The wood will absorb the force of the drill bit after it has gone through the metal.) Use a hand-held drill if you have a holder for it that creates a 90-degree angle between the drill bit and the silver-plated item. Forget trying to drill without a holder, because your drill bit will skitter around. If you are using a drill press, clamp the silver-plated item to the drilling platform base. Do not hold the item

in your hand. After drilling, file off any rough edges with a metal file.

We spruced up the drawers in the Studio kitchen by using flat table knives for the drawer pulls. They are a little harder to come by but worth the effort. A small, flat butter knife can also work for a smaller drawer.

5. Install on drawers or cabinets, using machine screws and spacers. Select the length of spacer based on how much room you will want for grabbing the handle.

Fork-and-Pot Place-Card Holders

Grace a garden party table setting with place-card holders made from tiny terra-cotta pots and forks. Or use them to identify buffet items or potluck dish ingredients.

Materials:

- Silver-plated forks
- Small terra-cotta pots, 2 inches or less in diameter
- 1 brick floral foam, such as Oasis
- 1 bag craft moss

Tools:

- Multipurpose rotary tool with cutting disc
- Locking pliers, such as Vise-Grips
- Safety goggles
- Glue gun

1. Cut the handle off each fork, leaving a 1-inch stub, using the rotary tool fitted with the cutting disc.

Hang on to the fork with pliers because the metal will get hot. Always wear safety goggles when cutting metal.

2. Fill the terra-cotta pots with floral foam to just below the rim. The foam is easy to cut with a serrated knife. The edges don't have to be perfect, but the foam needs to fit snugly in the pots.

3. Stick the stub end of a cut fork into the floral foam, up to the base of the fork.

4. Using the glue gun, apply glue to the foam and carefully press moss into it to hide the foam.

5. Stick a place card in the tines of each fork.

A garden party setting features enamelware containers, gear candlesticks, and place-card holders made from tiny terra-cotta pots. A utensil caddy is fashioned from a vintage glass holder that supports shiny tin cans—and allows you to be the hostess with the mostest.

Fork Pendant Necklace

This necklace looks best when your fork has four long, tapered tines, which gives you room to vary how you bend them. A varied design tends to look more interesting.

Materials:

- Silver-plated fork
- Jump rings in assorted sizes
- Jewelry chain with clasp (26 to 30 inches is an elegant length)
- Selection of charms or beads, each no more than 2 inches long

Tools:

- Vise or rubber mallet
- Wood, fabric, or leather scraps, if using a vise
- Multipurpose rotary tool with cutting disc
- Locking pliers, such as Vise-Grips
- Safety goggles
- Metal file
- Center punch

Twisty fork tines hold an abundance of treasured charms on this Fork Pendant Necklace.

- Hammer
- Hand-held drill or drill press
- $\frac{5}{64}$- or $\frac{3}{32}$-inch drill bit
- Countersink bit
- Smooth-nose pliers (preferred) or needle-nose pliers

1. Flatten the fork in a vise or with a rubber mallet. If you are using a vise, protect the fork between pieces of wood, heavy fabric, or leather. The fork doesn't have to be totally flat, but you want it to lie nicely against your neck.

2. Cut the handle off the fork, using the rotary tool fitted with the cutting disc. (Wear safety goggles while cutting and drilling.) The flat part of the fork and the tines will be left. Hang on to the fork with pliers because the metal will get hot.

3. Smooth the cut surface with a metal file. Some of the base metal will show through, but the contrasting metal color adds some interest to the fork.

4. Make a dimple in the cut end of the fork, approximately ¼ inch from the edge, with a center punch and hammer before you drill, so it won't bounce around.

5. Drill a hole from the front of the fork with your

hand-held drill or drill press, using a $5/64$- or $3/32$-inch drill bit. See "Drilling Silver Plate" for more information.

6. Smooth both sides of the hole with a countersink bit or metal file to remove the rough edges.

7. Grab one of the outside tines at the tip with the smooth-nose pliers and bend upward toward the top of the fork. If you bend in small increments and also move the pliers in small increments as you go, it will make a smoother curve. Curve it as much as you like.

8. Repeat with first the other outside tine and then the two inside tines. The curves can be similar or varied, with the tines bent to different degrees, but all of your tines should finish with a tight curl so that the jump rings cannot fall off.

9. Add a large jump ring to the top hole and hang the pendant on a piece of chain.

10. Add charms with jump rings to the curved tines.

Silverware Hooks

Spoons, forks, and serving utensils work best for this project. Shaping them around a dowel will keep the silverware from breaking and will give it an elegant bend. If your silverware does break, simply save it for another project, such as the pendant or place-card holder described earlier.

Materials:

- Silver-plated spoons or forks
- No.6 screws, ½ or ¾ inch long

Tools:

- Vise
- Rubber mallet
- Scraps of wood, heavy fabric, or leather, if using a vise
- Center punch, if using a spoon
- Hammer, if using a spoon
- Hand-held power drill or drill press, if using a spoon
- ⅜-inch drill bit
- Safety goggles, if drilling
- Countersink bit or metal file, if using a spoon
- Wooden dowel, ½ inches in diameter
- Screwdriver matching the type of screws you're using

Create an elegant spot to hold your keys, dog leash, or other special item. This cake server makes a sturdy hook.

1. Flatten a fork or spoon in a vise or with a rubber mallet. If you are using a vise, protect the silverware between pieces of wood, heavy fabric, or leather.

2. If using a spoon, make a dimple in the bowl with a center punch and hammer before you drill, so it won't bounce around. (Forks have a natural space between the tines for the screw, so drilling them isn't necessary.)

3. Wearing safety goggles, drill a hole in the bowl of the spoon with a hand-held drill or drill press, using a ⅜-inch drill bit. See "Drilling Silver Plate" earlier in this chapter for more information.

4. Smooth both sides of the hole with a countersink bit or metal file to remove the rough edges.

5. Bend the end of silverware around the dowel with your hand if you can. If this proves to be problematic, place the dowel and the silverware together in the vise and hit the silverware with the rubber mallet to curve it around the dowel. Keep in mind that you want the pretty face of the silverware's handle to be the front of your hook; this face should be on the outside of your bend. The front of the spoon or fork will face the wall or piece of wood, so bend the handle backward.

6. Attach the hook to your surface, using screws.

How to Display: A Guide to Arranging Your Collections (or How to Make Any Pile of Junk Look Amazingly Interesting!)

Time and time again, we hear from customers about how beautiful and inviting everything looks at the Salvage Studio—and they wish they could create the same artful displays at home. Well, you can, and it doesn't require anything special beyond what you already have in your house. All it takes is an understanding and application of some simple design principles.

Color, Function, and Form These are the three primary design principles that give you the foundation on which to build. Using at least one of these elements will give cohesiveness to any collection or "vignette," as we call the mixed displays we use at the Studio. In designing a vignette, assemble items that share the same color group, perform the same function, or reveal the same form or shape. Using more than one of these elements at a time will only add to a grouping's design strength.

Theme and Repetition Amy often combines a theme with one of the three design principles so that each display also tells a story. Common themes in her house include birds and flight, nature, time, and travel. In designing a themed vignette, remember that there is strength in numbers. Scattering items around a room diminishes their impact. A single item on a table or hung on a wall has no relation to anything else in the room and, unless it is very large or significant, will merely look random and inconsequential. Group items together so that your theme or story is evident, and repeat a pattern or combination within one room so that your decor flows together and has consistency.

Odd, Not Even Group items in odd numbers to lend a casual air to your display. Even numbers are symmetrical and thus tend to convey a more formal attitude. Have fun with your displays! Pair up quirky combinations, turn items upside down in one, make a pun or play on words in another. Engage the observer throughout the room with one or more senses.

Height and Texture Variations in height and texture also add dimension to your vignette. When the items are all the same height, it feels monotonous. Change the height of some items by placing them on a stack of books, the bottom of a bowl turned upside down, or a silver-plated pedestal (see the Serving Pedestals project in the Entertain chapter). Combine different textures for subtle visual variety. Add a rough texture, such as wood or fabric, to a display of smooth glass and metal, or add a shimmer of polished silver to an otherwise rusty-looking combination.

Change You don't have to display everything at once. Amy changes her home vignettes at least once a season, putting some items away and bringing out others. For more treasured mementos, such as a precious family photo, try changing its location, its grouping, or its prominence. This will always make it look fresh and loved in your home.

garden

The beauty of garden art is its ability to provide year-round interest, color, and structure to your outdoor spaces. Imagine, during the dreary days of late winter when you're itching to see something more cheerful than bare branches, catching a glimpse of a twinkling crystal chandelier or a cast-off birdcage painted a brilliant blue. Gracefully bent rebar stakes spiral in your dormant perennial beds. Two Adirondack chairs painted ocean blue add a punch of focus to the snow-

Lamp parts galore: In the forefront, two amber lamp globes add color and sparkle to the garden. A birdbath created from a combination of lamp pieces sits further back.

covered lawn. Peeking through some shrubs is a junk blossom composed from an old hubcap, wire petals, and broken china pieces (see the Junk Blossom project). And garden art is as low maintenance as it gets—no deadheading, watering, or weeding!

Believe in your garden style, whether minimalist or filled with details; there is no wrong or right way to style your garden. Decorate outside as you would inside: hang plates, set tables, use pillows. Or perhaps the inside of your home is all hustle and bustle, so you want to create a more serene escape outside. Follow your instincts. Your garden and the way you decorate it should make you happy—plain and simple.

Plates in the Garden

Plates are so versatile. You can quickly hang them on fences or lattice for more vertical interest. To secure plates to a fence, I use easy-to-find plate hangers from craft or dollar stores, along with a simple nail or screw for extra stability. To hang a plate on lattice, use an S hook. It slips simply over the lattice edge and creates the perfect hook to meet the plate hanger.

Use a variety of plates to create a garden edging with impact or to add a blast of oomph-filled color to a boring outside corner. My husband, Raoul, and I had eyes for a short granite wall, but our budget purchased cement blocks. The cement blocks gradually developed a lovely algae patina—fine progress, but not enough. In went a row of dinner plates to disguise the ugly blocks. Then one day while drying my hair, I had a brainstorm to layer the plates (heat to the brain can be quite useful!). I mixed together several solid colors and "stacked" them three deep, edge up: dinner plates in the back, salad plates in the middle, and bread plates up front.

Plates can also be used as filler between plants. In the beginning of my gardening career, I planted densely, wanting our garden to look full as quickly as possible. As middle age caught up with my lower back, the task of thinning out plants was absolutely unappealing. Now when I plant a new garden bed, I leave more room for the plants to expand, and in the meantime the bare earth can hold a nice selection of plates (or garden towers or garden tool signs or a gazillion possible combinations of found objects). As the garden plants fill out, the effect of the garden art becomes more subtle. And in time, when the plants don't want to share the space any longer, it is much easier to transplant a plate than a rhododendron.

Junk Art

We've all seen garden designs with found objects that give junk a bad rep. "Junk" is one of the best four-letter words we know (trumped only by "free"), but "junky" is not a word we want describing our gardens. Place your salvaged art to *complement* the plants, not to dominate or compete. Your garden plants should take top billing, and you should always have more plants than art.

———

A group of orphaned plates adorns a bedsprings garden trellis. A plain dinner plate can be punched up by gluing a smaller dish to the front of it.

Scale and Color

As you would indoors, create arrangements with your outdoor decorations. Small items can get lost outside, so group things together. When in doubt, use bigger pieces rather than smaller ones. There's no ceiling out in your garden, so your usual sense of scale needs to adjust.

Another way to amplify your displays and create cohesiveness with your outside styling is with color. Please don't be afraid of color! Brighter outdoor light will let you get away with more intense shades. Paint three things the same color—such as a pair of garden chairs, a small table, and a trellis—and spread them out a bit. The eye follows the color. Just as you repeat plantings, repeat the colors of your decorations. Capture attention with lighter colors; shades of white will be noticed first. If you want something to disappear, paint it dark green or black.

If you've ever painted the outside of your house, you probably learned how challenging it is to find the right shade of paint. What looks like a true shade of red when painted on a garden chair in your garage suddenly looks more pinkish out in full sunlight. My advice is to get over being upset or disappointed. It's just a garden chair, not your whole house, so live with it for a while. Sometimes you will like a happy mistake far more than your original idea.

Work the colors of the plants and the art off of each other. Sometimes you have established plants you are pleased with, but you'd like to spice them up a bit and draw more attention to them. For example, Raoul and I love hydrangeas. Except for looking like sticks in the winter, they are nearly perfect—easy care and months of amazing color that changes with the seasons. Our hydrangeas run the gamut from pinks and burgundies to creams and lots of blues. I've interspersed three tall garden towers containing all of those colors among a section of them. It's a stunning effect. The movement and textures of the hydrangeas contrast with the static, polished towers, while the towers naturally blend by mimicking the colors of the hydrangeas (see the Garden Dish Towers project).

Enhance your garden with delightful surprises. Mirrors are a charming addition when placed at different heights and locations in your garden, both drawing in light and reflecting it. (Be careful, however, of planting directly in front of mirrors, because tender foliage tends to burn in the intense reflected light.) Look for castoffs from bathroom remodels. They typically are really thick and will survive years in a garden if placed in a secure area. Don't worry about tiny chips or cracks around the edges; your plantings will soften and cover the edges in no time. It actually can be a relief to work with chipped, peeling, and rusty things. They have long ceased to be perfect. I have two large (3 by 4 feet) mirrors propped against a tall stone wall at the end of a path to create a fantasy window. You can also hang mirrors at eye level on a fence to frame the plants in front. Try painting the mirror frame a color that complements the plant it is highlighting. Small mirrors can dangle from tree branches. (If the light created by your mirrors is close to a neighbor's house, it's always a nice gesture to ask them if they mind the reflection.) And don't forget about placing mirrors at foot level, amid low plantings. Recently I found some side-view mirrors from a truck, with their brackets intact. Using the brackets as feet, I nestled the mirrors in a garden bed about a foot off the ground. They create pockets of light amid darker shrubbery and make the neighboring plants look fuller. On the down side, they can also make any bug damage look fuller, so put those mirrors behind the hostas the slugs *don't* dine on.

Other garden bling made from salvaged material includes sun catchers fashioned from silver-plated casserole holders, serving pieces, and cutlery; crystals; and some wire. Attach the pieces to each other with the wire and embellish them with as many wire loops and real crystal chandelier drops as you wish. Hung from a tree branch or your front door, it's a one-of-a-kind piece of art (see the Silver-Plated Sun Catcher project).

Another crowd pleaser involves adorning the edges of your patio umbrella. After coveting an expensive one I saw in a store, my envy gradually transformed into the idea of decorating the umbrella I already owned. I attached short strings of beads, with a chandelier crystal on the bottom of each, to earring hooks (the upside-down U-shaped style found at craft and jewelry supply stores). I then poked holes around the edge of the umbrella fabric with a large needle and inserted the earring hooks. An easy project for a dash of glamour.

Wind chimes of metal, pottery, or bamboo add aural depth to an area. Again, be considerate of your neighbors and place wind chimes closer to your house than to your property line. Water features produce visual as well as auditory pleasures. If the feature has moving water, experiment to find the right amount of flow. Most of us prefer to listen to a gentle bubbling or trickling rather than gushing.

It's crazy, but sometimes we actually use milk glass vases to hold real flowers (instead of salad dressings or buttons and wire flower-art pieces or...)!

Colorful garden tools and pots do double duty as garden decorations.

Another way to incorporate junk art in your garden is to create separate "rooms." Besides adding an element of mystery that lets your guests discover your garden space in stages, different physical areas help you incorporate all the elements you love that might not work if they were side by side. One garden section can be more delicate and formal, with garden towers and plates covering a fence. Another room might be highlighted with the more rusty, whimsical garden art you also love. Make little signs by planting rusty old tools with a stump of broken handle in the ground, with children's alphabet magnets attached. The use of rust in one part of your yard and silver plate in another creates contrast and interest.

Produce a Showstopper

Have something special in your garden that stops visitors in their tracks—not just a classic focal point, but a piece of garden art that makes visitors' hearts go pitter-pat. Besides delighting guests, an eye-catching piece of art can also divert them from another, less attractive element in the same space. Steps will quicken to admire a trio of garden towers or a stunning tall birdbath made from a floor lamp and dripping in crystals (see the Lampshade Birdbath project). No one will notice the gravel drainage ditch on an opposite wall or the holes in the hydrangea leaves from a recent hailstorm.

Concrete Fun

If you have partially used bags of concrete or mortar mix lying around, here's a great way to use them up: make perfectly formed cement balls, using round ceiling light-fixture globes. When placed in groupings in your garden beds or at the entrance to a path, the balls add an element of formal structure but unfussy texture. They can also be used as finials, candleholders, or even vases. The glass globes can typically be found at thrift stores and garage sales, often among the light fixtures. Gently clean the glass globe out with a damp rag and set it aside while you mix the concrete.

To mix concrete, put a small amount of water, about a gallon, in a wheelbarrow. Heave the bag of concrete directly into the wheelbarrow (it's easier than opening the bag, holding it in your arms, and pouring it in). Slice the bag open with a garden hoe, remove the paper wrapper, and then begin mixing the concrete with the hoe, using your body weight to drag the hoe toward you. Gradually add more water as needed. You want the mixture to look like thick fudge, not cream soup. When you don't see any more dry powder, you're ready to fill your glass molds. Press the concrete firmly into the glass globe for a smoother look, or press loosely for a rougher appearance.

To use a concrete ball as a candle holder or vase, fill the globe partway, then insert a glass votive holder or small bottle (for a vase) so that the top edge is flush with the rim of the globe. To make a finial, insert your decoration, such as a garden hand spade, submerging the handle in the concrete. Fill in more concrete around the insert until it is secure.

Let the filled molds dry for three days or so, depending on your weather. (If it's wet or cool out, dry them for a day or two longer.)

Now for the fun part—place one mold in a brown paper bag and *gently* whack it with a hammer. The glass will fall off of your newly minted cement ball. Mortar mix creates a very smooth finish resembling a bowling ball, while cement with gravel in it produces a more textured result. The balls can be painted with latex exterior house paint or left plain.

Discarded metal beds are priceless outside. The head and foot boards make terrific fencing or edging for a garden room, and the springs make really fine trellises. I have a double-size bedspring propped along a wall of my house. It's a sturdy and surprising trellis for a blooming vine, and it also provides great air circulation between the house and plant. When the vine is dormant, the springs are architecturally pleasing. And when it's time to paint the wall, I simply lean the bedspring away from the house. Choose a dark paint or stain for the wall to make the bedspring fade into the background. Rusty structures also nearly disappear visually underneath plants in full bloom.

You can plant, water, and weed and then find that

Mother Nature has another idea. Plants die. Bunnies show up and mistake your plants for a salad bar. Plants get wiped out by pets or family members. Found objects to the rescue! The first time Raoul and I were preparing for a local gardening group to tour our garden, we had a plant fatality. Instead of purchasing another plant, we covered the spot with a small blue footstool topped by a silver-plated candelabra and some vintage votive holders. We received so many compliments on this small vignette that it became a permanent feature.

Giving Function to Found Objects

Your garden art can be functional as well as decorative, such as the unique trellis described earlier constructed from rusty bedsprings. Rebar pieces can be bent into curlicues with a rebar bender to hold hanging plants, bird feeders, or lanterns or to act as stakes. Round bar

---

Sit—or Climb—and Admire

Design places to sit in the sun or shade to admire all your hard work. I try to sit in different areas of our garden to gain new perspectives for better placement of objects. It is also useful to see your outdoor space from a higher viewpoint. Look for a vantage point from which you can see as much of your yard as possible in one view: a window from an upper story of your home, a neighbor's upstairs window, a deck, or even your roof. With all the plants, garden rooms, and garden art distractions, you still want a cohesive and harmonious look for your entire outdoor space.

---

is smaller in diameter and so is easier to work with to achieve even more decorative designs. The heavier rebar, such as ⅜ inch, bends into gentle loops that keep your plants from flopping over as they bloom. Bells, beads, and wire can decorate your rebar stakes as well.

Other found objects that make useful garden stakes include these:

- Croquet mallets
- Machinery augers
- Chimney brushes
- Retired garden tools

Path edging can be formed from a row of ready-for-recycling glass bottles. Chardonnay wine bottles look fantastic side by side, with all their various green hues. At the end of a gravel path, I've placed a row of bottles sunken upside down into the dirt, with an inch of the bottle bottom still exposed. The gravel stays put, and it's easy to do. Simply dig a small trench, place the bottles upside down, side by side, and fill in the dirt. I like using cobalt-blue mineral-water bottles for this. You can also use this method with individual bottles to add spots of color in your garden path; the trick is to place them far enough out of the ground to be seen, but not tall enough to catch your toes on. Use a bulb planter to pop out the perfect section of dirt for the bottle's placement. Mine have been in the ground for several years, and not one has broken. Even if one does break, there's an easy solution—open up another bottle of wine, drink, and plant your empty!

Have fun with your garden art. It can be as simple as plopping colored bowling balls amid your plants. By the end of the growing season, they will have nearly disappeared as the plants fill in around them. Then in the depths of winter, there they are—loyal and true junk.

Lampshade Birdbath

This birdbath made from a recycled lamp fixture is functional as well as decorative. If you don't have a lamp finial for your final top screw, you can use a plain lamp nut and glue on your own decorative touch, such as a metal button or even a small glass dish. Chandelier crystals can be found at vintage lighting shops and the occasional antique shop, but I'll confess that I buy them new from a wonderful online source (www.freedom-crystal.com). Because each lamp varies in its design, it is quite handy to have some miscellaneous lamp parts on hand. Most lamp parts marry each other well.

Materials:

- Solid metal floor or table lamp base
- Decorative and sturdy bowl-shaped glass ceiling light-fixture shade (one with a hole in the middle)
- Chandelier crystals
- Clear, waterproof, and UV-resistant glue
- Small piece of plastic food wrap or plastic bag
- Lamp nut and washer (to fit standard threaded ⅛-IP lamp pipe)
- Any miscellaneous lamp parts you may have gathered over time, such as the metal spacer circles and decorative tube shapes that compose the top part of the lamp base below the socket
- Lamp finial (optional)

Tools:

- Wire cutters
- Chopstick

1. Disassemble the lamp by cutting the cord off at the lamp base, using wire cutters. Remove the socket by unscrewing it and/or gently popping it out of the socket base.

2. Unfortunately, you usually can't just place the ceiling lamp piece on the exposed threaded rod and be done with it. The empty socket space needs a little adjusting. You want 1 inch of bare threaded rod. Most lamp bases are composed of separate sections secured together with nuts on the top and bottom of the inside rod. The easiest solution is usually to

A table lamp base and a ceiling lamp globe transform into a gorgeous birdbath, sturdy enough to keep birds and gardeners alike happy.

remove a small spacer section from your lamp base to create the 1 inch of space needed for the glass lamp shade and finial. If your lamp has more than

This reinvented floor lamp can be moved to your seating area and used as a flower vase for entertaining; then returned to the garden to keep your bird friends supplied with fresh water.

1 inch of bare threaded rod exposed after the socket is removed, add a small section of lamp-base spacer tube. (If you don't have this stash of extra lamp parts, see the alternative instructions below.)

3. Place the light shade over the rod. You want about ¼ to ½ inch of rod exposed above the glass. It's a good idea to seal the base with glue. The threaded rod might be hollow, so stuff some plastic wrap or bag into the opening with a chopstick. Seal the inside of the rod with a squirt of glue. Add some glue in the space between the rod and the opening in the ceiling shade.

4. Place the washer and nut or finial on top and tighten it firmly.

Alternative instructions (if too much threaded rod is exposed and you don't have extra lamp spacers): On the inside of the bottom base, loosen the nut around the threaded rod that goes up through the main part of the lamp. Keep track of the order of the various lamp parts and arrange them in sequence as you remove them. By reassembling the lamp, you can sometimes get the parts to take up more room, shortening the length of the exposed rod on the top.

Silver-Plated Suncatcher

Made from two universally loved components—crystal chandelier drops and silver-plated dishes—these sun catchers brighten any garden space. Make yours as simple as a small silver-plated candy dish with a few crystals or as elaborate as a teapot suspended inside a casserole holder with all sorts of spoons and crystals in tiers surrounding it. Choose a casserole holder with a filigree edge; this provides built-in openings to string your wire through.

Materials:

- Silver-plated casserole holder, a 9- by 13-inch rectangle or 9-inch round
- Silver-plated pieces, such as gravy boat, sugar, creamer, candlestick, salt and pepper shakers, or cutlery
- About 5 yards silver-colored 20-gauge wire
- Chandelier crystals

A retired gravy boat now delights outside, suspended within a casserole holder and accented with elegant chandelier crystals.

Tools:

- Felt-tip pen
- Center punch or nail
- Hammer
- Drill press or hand-held drill with holder
- ⅛-inch drill bit
- Safety goggles
- Round-nose pliers
- Wire cutters

1. Lay out your composition of pieces.

2. If you are using cutlery, such as spoons and forks, a drill press is your best friend for drilling holes. You want them to be about an inch down from the tip of the handle. For knives, drill the handle, not the blade of the knife, which is far denser and harder to drill. Mark your chosen drill spots with a felt-tip pen. Make a dimple in the item at each drilling spot with a center punch or nail and a hammer. Wearing safety goggles, drill with a hand-held drill or drill press. See "Drilling Silver Plate" in the Look chapter for more information.

3. Select your focal point piece to attach first. Estimate how much wire to cut by eyeballing how far down you would like this piece to hang from the casserole holder and adding 24 inches more. Leaving a 12-inch tail, wrap and twist the wire around the top edge of the casserole holder where your focal point will hang. If you want lots of wire loops, use round-nose pliers to create a loop, twist, create a loop, and repeat until you run out of wire. (It's a good idea to practice a few loops on another piece of wire first. Your first loops will be okay, and the more you do, the smoother they will look. After another few, you'll feel comfortable making even more artistic wire flourishes.) For fewer loops, snip off some of the 12-inch tail. Attach the remaining straight piece of wire to your focal piece, wrap, and twist. Repeat the process for creating the wire loops.

4. You can attach the chandelier crystals to the wire loops and call it good or embellish your piece further by adding other small silver-plated pieces inside the casserole holder and/or suspended from your focal point piece. It's always a nice touch to add some wire and create lots of loops on the bottom end of the suspended casserole holder and suspend crystals there as well.

5. To hang your sun catcher, cut a piece of wire to create a hanger for the top. Usually the casserole holder still has its handles, and the top one is a handy place to attach your hanging wire.

If your garden art tastes lean more toward pretty than rustic, this is the project for you.

Garden Dish Towers

Made from all those china and glass dishes and vases that linger in the backs of our cupboards, these towers combine into pieces of garden art worthy of a spotlight location. Select a color theme and gather a variety of china and glass pieces in plain colors and patterns. Design your first tower to be about hip height; subsequent creations can be taller. For a stunning effect, design three towers of different heights in harmonious colors to be grouped together. Accept the fact that something probably will break before you finish. Be happy that you have more fodder for broken china mosaics—future garden stepping-stones!

Materials:

- Array of china, ceramic, and glass vases, cups, plates, bowls, cruets, and/or teapots—8 to 12 pieces
- Clear, waterproof, UV-resistant glue

Tools:

- Chopstick (optional)
- Small level
- Sharp craft knife for cutting, such as an X-Acto knife

1. Turn each piece upside down to see whether that is a more attractive presentation. Sometimes a piece such as a bowl looks prettier in your design with its opening facing down instead of up.

2. If you are using teapots, it's a good idea to seal the spout to keep water from collecting inside of it. Stuff a wad of plastic wrap into the spout with a chopstick and seal it with a dollop of glue.

3. Stack your pieces for a trial run. Do this when your pets are taking their naps. You'll want to start with a heavy piece with a large opening as your base, bottom side up. (A frostproof pot with a lovely glaze is ideal.) Stack pieces atop your base in segments. When possible, flip pieces, particularly plates, so the edges curve downward; that way, your tower collects less outdoor debris. Of course, plates look best right side up because the pattern is then visible, which is fine too. Salad and bread plates make handy transition pieces between larger or odd-shaped items. Save your most exciting piece for the top—the finial.

4. You're ready to start gluing your tower together, again in segments—maybe three or four pieces or

Add some va-voom to your yard or deck with a Garden Dish Tower. Smaller towers with a dinner plate for a base also work well and have instant stability.

fewer at a time. You'll quickly find out that china and glassware don't always have even surfaces. Use a small level and adjust the angle and placement of each piece as you go to avoid a Leaning Tower of Pisa.

5. If glue seeps out around the edges, wipe it away with a paper towel. You can also wait until it is totally dry and cut it away with a sharp craft knife.

6. Let your segments dry overnight. The following day you can glue your segments to one another.

7. Let the glue cure for at least 3 days.

8. To install your garden towers, you can partially bury short pieces of rebar in the ground. They can be only as tall as the height of your bottom piece—that pot with the wide opening. The rebar is not connected to your base but creates more stability. Make a nesting base of a layer of sand around the rebar and extending 2 inches beyond where your tower will sit. Place a circle of bricks around the perimeter of your tower base to stabilize it further. Add the circle of bricks only if your tower is placed toward the back of your garden bed and the neighboring plants will camouflage the bricks. Enlist a family member or friend to help you lift and carry the tower. Keep it as straight as possible when you move it.

9. Bring your piece in before the first frost.

Variation: Baby Garden Tower

If this looks like too much work, but you still like the dish tower idea, try making a Baby Garden Tower affixed over pieces of heavy (3/8- to 5/8-inch) rebar. These are much simpler versions of the freestanding towers. Select a clear, common florist's vase (10 to 12 inches tall)—the kind that is a dime a dozen at any thrift store—or go with a colored water or wine bottle for your base. Double-check that the mouth of the bottle will slide over the heavy piece of rebar. Then create a short tower consisting of three or four pieces of china and/or glassware together. Glue them together as described in the project instructions and let dry overnight. Glue your tower to the bottom of the vase or bottle. Since it can be a bit wobbly with no rebar supporting it, place the vase or bottle inside a pot or box for temporary support. Let the second round of glue cure overnight. Baby towers look best set on taller pieces of rebar (3 to 6 feet long) that are inserted 6 to 12 inches into the ground. Cluster three baby towers inside a large shrub so they are peeking out of the top, or use one in a potted container for a touch of whimsy.

Junk Blossom

These blossoms can live in your garden year-round. They produce a smile on your face in winter but don't need maintenance anytime of the year. If you haven't had a hubcap come loose recently, you can also layer two smaller metal pieces together, such as a cooling rack for baked goods and a pie plate.

Materials:

- 1 hubcap or 2 round metal pieces
- 14- or 16-gauge wire
- Beads, broken china or jewelry pieces, or flat glass marbles (1 to 2 dozen)
- Clear, waterproof, UV-resistant glue
- Long wooden handle from a broken tool like a rake or mop (approximately 4 to 5 feet long)
- Two ½-inch wood screws

Tools:

- Heavy 2-inch nail
- Hammer

1. If you are using two metal rounds as your blossom center (or "eye"), first secure these together with a few pieces of wire through any existing openings that are as close to the center as possible. Twist the wires closed

A fanciful Junk Blossom plays off of the neighboring plants but it steals the show with its whimsy and carefree ways.

on the back side. If necessary, punch holes for the wires near the center of the pieces, using a hammer and nail.

2. If there are no holes or openings near the edges of your hubcap or other metal pieces where your petals will be attached, make your own with a hammer and nail. The holes need only be big enough to slip your wire through.

3. Determine where the back center part of your round metal piece will attach to the stake. The stake will

Inside Out, Outside In

Garden art made from salvaged materials often looks as good inside your home as it does outside. From the dining room table to your perennials bed, real lead crystals and porcelain dishes are beautiful *and* frost proof. The serving pedestals shown in the Entertain chapter can be stacked up and left outside for display or grouped together individually with candles for outdoor lighting. You'll find that some silver plate will start to rust (which is a wonderful development, in my opinion); just leave it outside for a shorter period if you want to retain more silver than rust. Likewise, a Garden Dish Tower composed of clear glass dishes and vases with a large bowl on top can go from being a lovely birdbath outside to a whimsical candleholder inside (with a lavish rinse of vinegar and water to prepare it for inside/people use). The Lampshade Birdbath can come inside for the fall and winter to hold candles or flowers for a party. Or fill it with pinecones or baby pumpkins for a charming display. For the holidays, use a generous heap of holiday ornaments.

have two wood screws attached for your contact points. If the center of your metal piece has no openings or holes, create two holes by punching a heavy nail through the metal with your hammer for the final connecting piece of wire (see step 6).

4. Your blossom petals are loops of twisted wire. You can fashion free-form loops by hand or wrap your wire around a wooden dowel or a broom handle. If your petals are big and loopy (and I encourage you to do big and loopy), attach them by wrapping the wire ends around the holes you made previously in the edges of your round metal piece, one at a time.

Who wouldn't want to nestle into one of these chairs and have a refreshing drink of lemonade? An old, faded sun umbrella gets new life from crystal embellishments and is a perfect complement to a Junk Blossom and Baby Garden Towers.

5. Embellish your blossom by hanging beads from the wires with small pieces of wire or gluing pieces of broken china or jewelry or flat glass marbles to sections of the round metal piece. Look in your junk drawer or that jar of miscellaneous metal stuff in your garage for other possible enhancements.

6. To attach your blossom to its stem, the broken tool handle, screw two wood screws into the top portion of the handle, about 4 and 6 inches down from the top. Use a section of wire to connect the blossom to the two screws by first threading your wire through the openings in the hubcap as close to the back center of the hubcap as possible. Holding the back of the blossom to the side of the stake that has the screws, wrap the wire ends around the screws several times. Wrap any of the leftover wire ends around the handle for further stability. The junk blossom will be top-heavy, so be sure to insert its "stem" into the ground at least 6 to 12 inches.

LISA

refresh

I find that just saying the word "refresh" out loud elicits an instant relaxation response in me. Breathe in on the first syllable and breathe out on the last, and you will see what I mean. We don't take enough time out for ourselves. It is a cultural crisis and our daily challenge to make time and create spaces to refresh our body, mind, and spirit. Plan ways to get away from the phone, work, and other busyness. Schedule breaks if you have to. This is especially important if you work from home or are a caregiver or parent, in which case there is no official quitting time and certainly no official breaks.

Getting outside during the day helps smooth frayed nerves, and breathing in fresh air clears the cobwebs out of your brain. Beth uses a 20-minute jaunt around her neighborhood to refresh her mind. Even if she starts off stewing over something, she quickly gets distracted by listening to the birds, looking at the clouds, and seeing what new plant is blooming.

Birds of a Feather

I use the garden year-round to refresh and recharge after spending the morning creating or tending to business on the computer. My garden has been a Backyard Wildlife Sanctuary since 1993. By creating an oasis for wildlife,

———

Fresh lemonade served in pint-sized canning jars instantly says "summer." For a serving tray, insert a piece of pretty paper or embroidered linen into an old picture frame.

Doug and I have also created an oasis for ourselves. Bird feeders and butterfly-friendly plants entice fauna to visit the garden—providing instant stress relief on a busy day. One of my favorite bird feeders is one Beth created from an old Christmas-tree stand. The vibrant red of the metal stand, combined with the ready-made bowl, provide a winning combination for the birds and the garden (see the Tree-Stand Bird Feeder project).

Adorn a birdhouse with bits and baubles you have around the house. This creation sparkles with decorative half marbles that are typically used in flower vases or in mosaics.

One of the criteria of a Backyard Wildlife Sanctuary is having berries and fruit for wildlife to eat. Fortunately, most are edible for us, too. I spend a few minutes each day grazing in the garden, looking for a blueberry here or a raspberry there. A wild strawberry groundcover produces small, delicious berries too. It's an easy way to grab a handful of antioxidants, and the taste of fresh fruit warmed by the sun is good for my soul.

No matter how busy her day, Amy always tries to stop what she's doing and have lunch. Sounds like an easy thing to do, right? But it often takes a conscious effort to sit down, eat something, and take a few moments to register on the day. I like to eat lunch outside, watching my chickens Nugget and Noodle peck and scratch around the garden. (They're always interested in what is on my menu; pasta and rice are favorites.) Doug made a henhouse for the girls, all from recycled materials. The siding is from the free pile at a local construction salvage company, and the shingles are leftovers from an Oregon farmhouse. In fact, the chickens are recycled too! My cousin Summer was moving to Romania and was looking for adoptive parents for her beloved flock.

Of course, not everyone can have chickens to enhance the backyard experience! But add birdhouses and plants that provide shelter in your garden, and you will have feathered friends galore.

Timeless Pieces

The garden rooms that Beth describes in the Garden chapter can be perfect spots to relax and unwind. Using recycled and weathered materials in the walls and surfaces of such a space gives a sense of timelessness to the garden that can enhance your mood for reflection.

Backyard Wildlife Sanctuary

With a few simple steps, you can register your own garden as a Backyard Wildlife Sanctuary. You need to provide shelter, food, and water for wildlife and maintain good organic gardening practices. Visit the National Wildlife Federation website at www.nwf.org to register your garden.

My friend Karen lives in her grandmother's home and several years ago cleared out some of the old garden debris. She asked me if I would like any of the objects, and I was immediately drawn to two pieces of a 70-year-old wooden arbor, the chipped white patina aged to perfection. This arbor was original to the house, circa 1939. I carefully removed the rot from the bottom of the support posts of the arbor panels and gave them new, sturdy uprights that could safely be sunk in the ground. They became the entrance walls to what I call our Sunset Garden. In the pile of Karen's garden salvage was also a single section of the existing curved arbor top that we then attached to the two pieces of wall—like icing on a cake. The first time Beth visited my garden, she made me promise to leave the arbor sections to her in my will. Karen was surprised and pleased by the arbor's renewed life, and in homage to her grandmother, I planted yellow daffodils along both sides of the wall because Karen remembered that every spring during their Easter egg hunts, her grandmother's arbor walk was lined with daffodils.

Even if you don't have access to splendid salvaged architectural pieces, you can easily create age and inter-est in your favorite refuge by using found objects. One of the simplest ways to do this is to make signs featuring words that resonate for you, such as "joy," "grow," or "nest." Form the letters from a variety of found objects, like metal rings and rods, iron scraps, horseshoes, oarlocks, or even sticks and pebbles. Decorate your garden spot or cozy reading corner with these signs to reinforce your mental change of pace.

Sit for a Spell

Places to sit in the garden are crucial for me and my daily renewal time. Even just a slight break and change of scenery often spark a new idea or solution to a problem. I find that I then have more energy to continue my day.

In our Sunset Garden, Doug and I have refreshed some old resin chairs I rescued from the dump by painting them with a plastic spray-paint product. That was three years ago, and they still look great. I admit I'd prefer a pair of lovely wooden Adirondack chairs, but the ability to rescue and salvage things gives me a different type of satisfaction and pleasure. The resin chairs were elevated to a more designer look when I painted three salvaged metal birdcages the same color as the chairs and hung them from nearby trees. Add a retired pancake griddle to the top of a rusty metal birdcage, and you have an instant side table.

Another area of our garden features a bench we built from old hunks of concrete, brick, and found objects. For the cost of three bags of instant concrete we used as mortar, we have a lovely place to sit and rest that will be a focal point in our garden for years to come. But our favorite seat by far is the Three-Chairs-in-a-Row Bench. I found four metal chairs rusting in the back-forty of our garden, along with a fallen-down and rotting wooden

Water, Water Everywhere

Any curved rock or saucer can be a welcome watering hole for birds and butterflies. Many beneficial wasps and bees need water, too, to make mud for their hives to help insulate and protect their young. Placed upside down on a pedestal, even a galvanized garbage-can lid can provide an instant birdbath. In my front garden, I have a concrete birdbath that I found on the side of the road on trash pickup day, presumably because there is a chunk broken off of one edge. But it still holds water, and the birds don't seem to mind the defect. A favorite quick birdbath of mine is a terra-cotta pot turned upside down with the pot's saucer set on top. It's easy to move and keep clean, it looks good in the garden, and the materials are readily available.

garden gate. We combined the best pieces of these items to create a bench that is sturdy enough for the outdoors but elegant enough to grace an entry of a home (see the Three-Chairs-in-a-Row Bench project).

Bring the Outdoors In

If you don't have a garden or are unable to create and maintain one, you can still derive the refreshing benefit of the outdoors. Decorate with floral pillows or fabrics; use found nests or feathers as accents; look for floral-motif paintings at thrift stores; place a bouquet of fresh flowers on your table or a vase of culinary herbs in your kitchen window. I designed my garden so that I can see it and take it all in from the house, even if the weather

doesn't cooperate. Create a cozy indoor spot with an outdoor vista that appeals to you.

You can also borrow someone else's outdoor refuge. I have been a member of a local organic farm, the Root Connection, for about 10 years. The Root Connection is the oldest community-supported agriculture (CSA) endeavor in Washington State. I pick up our weekly share of produce at the farm, as well as fresh-picked flowers and herbs, in return for a yearly membership fee. Spending time at the farm is one of my weekly highlights. Each week the gardens look different, with something new to explore and admire. The shared sense of community is palpable. Watching young children pluck their first carrot from the ground provides a simple sense of renewal. And the fresh air is a tonic. Even a stormy, cloudy day at the farm is invigorating, and I return home, laden with fresh vegetables and fresh inspiration for dinner. If you don't have access to your own CSA, visit a local farmer's market or you-pick farm to bring home that farm-fresh feeling.

Other borrowed outdoor spaces include neighborhood parks, waterfront piers, community gardens, and rooftop decks. Or simply walk across the street and join your neighbor on her front porch.

Recharging the Home

One thing I've learned the hard way is that my surroundings often reflect my mind. An organized, restful room induces the same in my mental state. During

To highlight favorite pieces, use a stack of interesting old books as a pedestal, or turn over a glass urn as a cloche. Even a chunk of salvaged architecture or a pair of aged scissors can add intrigue to a display.

some of the more prolific salvaging episodes for the Studio, parts of my home became disorganized and chaotic, and that was reflected in my mental and spiritual well-being. I now make a daily, conscious effort to create a spot of beauty in each area of my home, so my eyes and mind have a place to rest, a respite from the chaos from morning to night.

I also like to refresh and decorate my front porch according to the seasons or holidays. There is nothing like a literal clean sweep to recharge you and your home. A swept and tidy front porch sets the tone for the rest of the house. If you have only a few minutes, knock the cobwebs down from the eaves, set a small table beside the front door, and add a fresh bouquet. Even if the rest of the place looks like a tornado hit, the crisp entry will perk you up and bring a smile to your visitor's face.

By my front door is a table on top of which I have a treasured piece of rusty metal—a hoe bit made by my father-in-law that I salvaged from his Oregon farm. Magnetic letters from a tossed children's toy spell the word "grace" across its aged red surface, but the sentiment changes with the seasons and my mood. In October it might say "boo," and during December it says "ho ho ho" (of course!). "Refesh" and "renew" are other popular words I use. Pausing to read this simple message as I enter my home alters my mindset and

(Left) The broken, rusty blade of a garden hoe holds children's magnets conveying a sweet thought. It rests on a particularly wonderful rusty piece, now part of a Metal-Gear Candlestick. (Right) Casually scattered stamps brighten this silver-plated tray like confetti. Place shells and stones in a jar for a simple yet interesting display. The recycled beakers are awaiting flowers or wine—hostess's choice.

eases the tone of each day.

Beth creates seasonal displays in her front entryway, while Amy changes the decor throughout her home with each new season. We can get into a decorating rut; changing things around refreshes a room and inevitably inspires our minds.

Calming Companions

One thing we have in common at the Salvage Studio is our love for our companion animals. We all agree that sharing our homes with pets has taught us some lessons about living a balanced life. Their needs are simple and their affection unconditional; they are always focused on what is important—eating, sleeping, playing, and

Play with Bloggers

Sometimes our sense of creative play needs a boost, and the Internet offers a gold mine of inspiration and ideas. Reading your favorite blog can spark creativity, as well as open your mind to new and wonderful people, places, and things. Beth is the avid blog reader among us. Her favorites feature lots of eye candy, such as vintage ephemera, glitter, jewelry, and paper arts.

Here are our top five blogs for inspiration:

- Posie Gets Cozy, by Alicia Paulson (rosylittlethings.typepad.com/)
- Tongue in Cheek, by Corey Amaro (willows95988.typepad.com/)
- Pam Garrison (pamgarrison.typepad.com/)
- Crazy Aunt Purl, by Laurie Perry (www.crazyauntpurl.com/)
- Simply Green, by Danny Seo (dannyseo.typepad.com/)

loving. For instance, cats have no trouble taking time out to just sit and relax, preferably on an available warm lap. (When one of our cats is sleeping on his lap, my husband, Doug, says he's "taking his blood pressure medicine.") Amy has taken this furry example to heart: for more than 30 years, she has benefited from a 10- to 15-minute catnap almost every afternoon, and she is still amazed at the rejuvenating quality. Beth's approach is more catnip than catnap: one of her favorite things to do to regroup is to stop and kiss one of her cats' furry tummies.

Pets teach us that you don't need a lot to be happy and have fun. Amy's loyal friend Forrest, a golden retriever, had a favorite toy they called Baby made from an old T-shirt tied in knots. Forrest's successor, Calvin, has carried on the toy tradition. And with T-shirts so easy to find at garage sales and thrift stores, and in your own closet, you and your pet are guaranteed hours of fun.

My cats love to perch up high, as do most indoor felines. We devised a fun area for them in the family room, using small wooden kids' chairs mounted to the wall, Shaker style. The mounted minichairs provide ladderlike shelves for climbing and perching and lead up to a shelf mounted over the door into the room. The cats climb up and survey their domain while we relax in the evenings.

For Beth, Amy, and me, the art of creating and playing around with materials and decor is gratifying. Whether it's inventing a new pasta recipe, stringing beads into a necklace, or displaying seemingly unrelated found objects together, some brand-new idea always emerges and delights. Assembling different components into a piece of garden art or home decor results in a tangible effort that is also a restful act. (Something from nothing, inventing without demands—it's addictive!) Time spent in your garden oasis, your shared community, or your home refuge is also a time to pause and clear your mind. You will gain a new perspective and increased energy and be able to face the rest of your day refreshed.

Three-Chairs-in-a-Row Bench

I found four metal kitchen chairs on the side of the road, destined for the dump. When I married three of them to two wooden slats from an old garden gate I had been hanging on to for years (waiting for just the right project!), a one-of-a-kind garden bench was born. The chairs can be made of wood or other materials, but metal holds up best outside, and while they can be different in style and color, the seat height needs to be the same.

Materials:

- 3 kitchen chairs
- Indoor/outdoor spray enamel paint (optional)
- Wooden boards to span the length and width of your chairs
- No.8 wood screws long enough to go through the chairs and partway through the boards, 2 to 3 inches long (save screws from existing chair cushions if they are still good)

Dress up a garden bench like this one with an inviting backdrop. We used rusty bedsprings against a common fence to create depth and visual interest. Hang a few decorative plates; add a birdhouse, a water fountain, or pots of flowers for a "welcome home" treat.

Tools:

- Phillips head screwdriver
- Measuring tape
- Pencil
- Circular saw or jigsaw
- Safety goggles
- Medium- and fine-grit sandpaper
- Hand-held power drill
- ⅜-inch drill bit

1. Remove the seat cushions from the chairs (salvage the screws if they're still good). If you want to paint the chairs a uniform color, now is the time.

2. Place the three chairs side by side and measure the total length. Mark this length on the boards with a pencil, and cut the boards to length with a circular saw or jig-saw. (Wear safety goggles when cutting and drilling.)

3. Sand the boards, if necessary, to remove chipped or peeling paint, smooth the rough edges, and remove potential splinters from the seating area.

4. Place the boards upside down on a long table or other surface, and then place the chairs upside down on the boards in their final spot.

5. Drill through the existing holes in the chairs where the old seat cushions were attached, partway into the boards, or drill pilot holes, two on each side, if the chairs didn't originally have seat cushions. Be careful to drill only partway through the boards. Don't go all the way through.

6. Use salvaged screws or new wood screws to attach the chairs to the boards.

7. Place right side up and enjoy your new bench.

Tree-Stand Bird Feeder

The classic red metal holiday tree stand, with the green metal legs, is nearly a staple in the secondhand world. They are usually in great shape because they didn't work very well holding up that heavy tree, but now they have a second chance as a useful and colorful bird feeder.

Materials:

- Bowl from a metal tree stand
- Sturdy 54-inch chain (links should be approximately ½ to 1 inch long)
- 2 yards 16- or 18-gauge wire
- 2 or 3 red glass dishes, such as a candleholder, bowl, bread plate, and/or vase (pieces should total 4 to 6 inches in height)
- Clear, waterproof, UV-resistant glue
- Shepherd's hook or 12-inch L-shaped bracket with curved end for hanging (optional)

Tools:

- 2 pairs heavy-duty pliers—lineman's pliers if you have them
- Wire cutters
- Round-nose pliers

1. Most tree stands come assembled, but it's easy to take them apart. There are typically three eye screws to unscrew. Once they are removed, the legs will slip away from an O-shaped piece of metal in which the red bowl sits. Save the screws for a future project. The metal O is perfect for a junk sign letter (see the Junk Word Sign project), and the metal legs are easy to save, too, because they stack together. Next time you see us, ask if we've figured out what to do with them yet.

2. Separate the chain into three equal pieces approximately 18 inches in length. We're always on the lookout for swag lamps because in addition to the funky light parts, they come with oodles of sturdy chain. It is extremely hard to cut. An easier route is to separate the links by using heavy pliers or lineman's pliers in each hand to swivel the link apart.

3. The tree stand bowl will have three holes around the rim. Cut a 12-inch piece of wire, thread it through one of these holes, and attach a piece of chain by looping it through a link and twisting the wire closed three times. Using round-nose pliers, make little loops with the wire tails as a decorative touch, if you wish.

4. When all three pieces of chain are attached, cut a 24-inch length of wire. Thread it through the top link of each chain, with the ends of the wire even, and secure them together by twisting the wire closed three times. To form a hanger, move 6 inches away

from the first wire twist, and secure the wire ends together by twisting three times. For one last decorative detail, use the round-nose pliers to make more little loops with the wire tails. Separate the 6-inch expanse of wire between the twists to form an oval for hanging.

A Tree-Stand Bird Feeder joins other fun garden items, including rescued rakes turned into tool holders and crystal mini Garden Towers.

5. With the mechanics all squared away, now it's time to cover those sharp prongs in the center of the tree stand bowl. Select two or three pieces of red glassware and glue them together into a 4- to 6-inch tower. The bottom piece should be broad enough to cover the prongs. Glue this little tower to the metal bowl. This structure also provides the birds an additional perch. Allow the glue to dry for several days before installing the bird feeder outdoors.

6. To hang your bird feeder, slip the wire hanger loop over a tree branch, suspend it from a very sturdy shepherd's hook placed in a garden pot or flower bed, or attach a 12-inch L-shaped bracket with a curved end to a wall for hanging the feeder.

Chickadee Birdhouse

We love having chickadees nest in our garden and get several families from our nesting pair each summer in the chickadee house we've mounted under our carport. With a few guidelines and pieces of scrap lumber, you can create a haven for our feathered friends. See "Build a Better Birdhouse" for more information and ideas.

Materials:

- Scrap lumber (1-by-6s will do)
- 1⅛-inch finishing nails
- Bits and pieces of hardware and wood for decoration
- No.10 tin can (the size used in restaurants)
- No.8 wood screws, ½-inch or ¾-inch

Tools:

- Ruler
- Pencil
- Table saw, circular saw, or jigsaw
- Safety goggles
- Drill press or hand-held power drill
- 1⅛-inch keyhole drill bit
- ³⁄₁₆-inch, ⅜-inch, and ½-inch drill bits
- Work gloves
- Tin snips
- Needle-nose pliers

Welcome home, chickadees! This delightful birdhouse was made for Lisa by her family. The miniature window box is made from the lid of the tin can used for the roof and "planted" with dried flowers from her mother's garden.

1. Gather your scrap lumber, making sure no toxic chemicals have been used on the wood. It is not necessary to preserve the wood in any way.

2. Cut the pieces of the birdhouse, using a table saw, circular saw, or jigsaw. (Wear safety goggles when cutting and drilling.) The floor will be 4 by 4 inches. The back will be 4 by 10 inches tall at the peak. You can make a peak by cutting a 4- by 10-inch rectangle of wood, marking the center point on the top, and cutting from the center to the side at a 45-degree angle. Assuming that your wood is ¾ inch thick, the front will be 10 inches tall and 5½ inches wide. That's the 4 inches of the floor plus the thickness of the two sides. The sides are 4¾ inches wide, which allows them to extend far enough to cover up the back, and 7¼ inches tall.

3. Using a drill fitted with a 1⅛-inch keyhole bit, cut a hole in the front piece 6 to 8 inches above the bottom.

4. Drill a hole in the back with a ½-inch drill bit so you can hang your birdhouse later.

5. Loosely put your house together and mark where you will drill a few pilot holes. I recommend three pilot holes along the sides of the front piece and two along the bottom of the front piece. They should be about ¼ inch from the bottom and the sides so that they go into the side and bottom pieces of wood. Drill these holes with the 3⁄16-inch drill bit; it should be slightly smaller than the size of your finishing nails.

6. Repeat on the back piece.

7. Now use finishing nails to nail the birdhouse together. Don't worry if you have gaps and it doesn't all fit together flush. You are making a rustic birdhouse.

8. Now is the time to embellish. You can add wooden doodads or metal hardware or anything you can imagine.

9. Take a clean No.10 tin can with both the top and bottom removed and cut it in half from top to bottom with tin snips. Wear work gloves because the edges will be really sharp. Flatten the metal, determine the middle, place it against the edge of a sturdy table or other edge, and press down to make the peak of your roof. Place the tin roof on the birdhouse and mark eight places for pilot holes for screws: two on each side, front and back. Make sure the back of the roof is flush with the back of the birdhouse so it will rest against the wall or fence you hang it on. Remove the tin roof and drill the holes in the can, using the 3⁄8-inch drill bit. Place the roof over the house again and mark where you will drill pilot holes in the wood. Remove the roof, drill the holes, and attach the roof with wood screws.

10. Using tin snips, make cuts approximately 2 inches long along the bottom edges of the metal roof. Using needle-nose pliers, curl the edges up to make a gingerbread edge.

11. Hang the finished birdhouse in your garden in a sheltered spot and enjoy the families of birds that will live there for years to come.

Junk Word Sign

I made this "joy" sign for Beth for Christmas one year. It's now part of her holiday front-porch display. Hang it on a garden gate, use it to grace an entryway, or place it outside your kitchen window for inspiration.

What you use as letters will make your statement. For Beth's "joy" sign, I used a rusty iron farm hook to make the "J." The "O" is the top of a Christmas-tree stand, and the "Y" is a pruning from a yellow-twig dogwood.

Some ideas for letters: The poker end of a fireplace tool makes an excellent lowercase "r"; horseshoes are an easy "U," "C," or lowercase "n"; and big rusty washers are a classic "O." Take old bicycle chain, shape it into your letters, and leave outside to rust into shape.

Offering delightful sentiments for indoors or out, Junk Word Signs make wonderful gifts.

Once your letter materials are set, select your background board. I used a piece of old fascia from our house that had several layers of old blue-green paint.

Materials:

- Long, rectangular piece of wood to mount letters on (the size will be determined by your word choice)
- Letters to spell your chosen word (made of metal, twigs, wood, or any combination)
- 18-gauge copper wire
- 1 foot of 18-gauge galvanized wire
- Old hinge
- Screws to fit hinge and partway through the wooden backing

Tools:

- Table saw, circular saw, or jigsaw
- Medium- and fine-grit sandpaper
- Safety goggles
- Pencil
- Hand-held power drill or drill press
- 3/16-inch drill bit
- Wire cutters
- Needle-nose pliers
- Screwdriver to match the screws for the hinge

1. Using your chosen saw, cut the piece of wood to fit your letters, leaving a border of at least 3 inches on either side of the word. (Wear safety goggles when cutting with power tools.) Sand off any chippy bits of paint. If you don't have a previously painted piece of wood, make your own by painting a couple of colors on a piece of old fence board; let the coats of paint dry thoroughly between applications, and then sand.

Depending on the look you want, any old, weathered piece of wood without paint would be great.

2. Place the letters on the board and, using a pencil, mark where the holes will go to attach the letters to the board. You will make homemade staples out of the copper wire to hold the letters in place. For instance, to attach the "J," I had a hole on either side of the upright leg of the letter and a hole on either side of the lower part of the hook. Think ahead to what gravity will do to the letter when the sign is hung up.

3. Using your marks, drill holes all the way through the wood with a drill press or hand-held drill, using a 3/16-inch drill bit.

4. Cut pieces of copper wire about 6 inches long to use as staples.

5. Place your first letter back in position, bend a piece of wire into a U shape, and place both ends into the holes on either side of the letter. Push the wire through until it is flush in front, or make it as tight as you can. Push the second "staple" through the second attachment point on the letter.

6. Hold the letter in place and flip the sign over.

7. Use needle-nose pliers to pull the wire tightly through from the front and create a bend in the wire flush with the back. Twist the ends together tightly. Continue attaching the rest of the letters in this manner.

8. When you are done, attach the hinge to the center of the top of the back with the screws to make a hanger. If you have half a hinge, run the galvanized wire through the pin slots. If you have a whole hinge, run the wire through the second set of screw holes. Twist the ends of the wire together to form a loop for hanging. If your board is long, use a hinge at each end.

Build a Better Birdhouse

At the Studio, one of our most popular workshops is Rustic Birdhouses. We supply the class with chickadee-specific birdhouse kits and some general assembly directions, and then the hammering begins. We provide lots of interesting items to embellish the houses: wooden spindles cut in half; slices of children's alphabet blocks, model train track, wooden yardsticks, and rusty old hardware.

Any salvaged wood can be used as long as it hasn't been finished with a toxic chemical such as wood preservative or soaked with oil. Plain old cedar fencing is an excellent choice. The use of No.10 tin cans for the roofs was inspired by my parents, who made a birdhouse years ago that is still lovingly displayed in my dining room. They used a tin can for the roof, and Mom clipped the edges with tin snips and curled them up like a flip hairstyle. It looks like a Pippi Longstocking hairdo! If this birdhouse was placed out in the garden, the roof would rust up nicely. Old cedar shingles or vintage license plates also work well for the roofs. Just make sure you attach the roof with screws so that you can easily remove it to clean the house out annually. If you don't, bees or wasps will move in and drive the birds away. My friends Richard and Nancy cleaned out all their birdhouses on Valentine's Day one year, and I thought that was an excellent way to remember; it's too early for birds to have begun nesting yet but late enough in our climate that winter shelter isn't so crucial.

Patterns for birdhouses are plentiful in woodworking magazines and books, but be aware that while they may look great, birds may not come to live in them. I recommend deciding what birds you want to attract to your garden and then building the house specifically for that variety. The size of the hole, where it is positioned on the front of the house, the floor dimensions, and where the house is located in the garden all play a part in the birds' decision to move in and raise a family.

Contrary to popular belief, birdhouses don't need perches. In fact, predator birds often use them to sit on and pluck the baby birds out of the house. If you experience problems with predators, you can make a hole extender by cutting the appropriate-size hole in a block of wood and placing it over the existing entrance hole. Attach it to the front of the house with screws. This creates a deeper entrance hole, making it harder for the predator bird to get its neck in the house. The parent bird cares only about the proper-size hole, not how deep it is.

In our garden, we have houses to attract chickadees and wrens because we love watching them feed their young and we love the songs they sing all year long in the garden. Our chickadee houses are located on the east and north sides of our house. It keeps them sheltered from the intense sun. The babies would overheat anywhere else; the parent birds realize this and avoid houses in the full sun.

entertain

A favorite quote of mine comes from Virginia Woolf: "One cannot think well, love well, sleep well, if one has not dined well." Certainly, the enjoyment of good food, especially in the company of friends and family, is a pleasure for many. But good entertaining is about so much more than food. A lively atmosphere and engaging setting contribute to an event, whether large or small, and make both the guest and host feel comfortable and satisfied.

Though happy accident often plays a part, it also takes only a little effort to plan such a gathering if you

Pressed glass and silver-plated dishes combine to form unique candle pedestals.

are already in the Salvage Studio mode. First of all, plan the event you would want to attend; it's important for the host to have fun at her own party. Invite people you care about, prepare food that you enjoy eating, and create activities that you want to do. During the party, look out for the needs of your guests, introducing them to one another, finding a moment to talk with each person, and making everyone feel at ease. Your enthusiasm will be contagious and encourage a convivial atmosphere.

Setting the Tone

We all want to share everyday moments, special events, and annual holidays with our friends and families because it adds more meaning to our lives, more depth. It brings

happiness and satisfaction to show them that we care. The invitation is the first introduction to this impulse; it sets the tone for your gathering. An invitation doesn't have to be elaborate. Even a simple invite can show more thought than an e-mail or a telephone message.

Often the plainest of items can convey just the right party spirit. An old bingo card is the ideal weight and size to act as a postcard invitation. Jot a quick note on the reverse, add an address and stamp, and you're done. This invitation was perfect for an afternoon open house where board and card games were the focus of activity.

Plain paper bags can be used to make a variety of invitations. For a recent birthday party, I bound together three small paper bags on their closed ends, using a needle and thread. Each bag opening held a paper insert that included the party details, a map to the location, and RSVP info. To better communicate the festive atmosphere I planned, I glued a scrap of wrapping paper to the front bag and embellished it with rubber stamps, a snippet of ribbon, and a few beads.

Style has nothing to do with money, and you don't need to have fancy stemware to serve your guests. An assortment of glasses, matching or varied, fits the salvage style. I have collected a number of vintage jelly glasses, all of them rimmed with embossed stars. Glass tumblers like these are perfect for a party because you can use them for soda or iced tea or wine. Think Italian trattoria and bring that same continental flair to your own setting. I've also found that small salad or dessert plates work best for buffets; dinner plates are too large

Lamp Candleholders made from assorted lamp and metal salvage provide candlelight, while old photos displayed in jars atop a salvaged wood pedestal add to the intimacy.

Old Forks

Old forks that are too worn or bent to use for food can be turned into other entertaining extras. A lone silver-plated fork holding a game-card letter gives a playful clue as to whose seat this might be. You can either insert the game card among the tines and set the fork at the place setting or turn the fork into a miniature easel (see the Fork Easels project in the Look chapter) to hold the card in place. Instead of place cards, use these mini-easels to either label food at the buffet table or provide information to party participants.

and heavy. They're easy to acquire in sufficient quantity by picking up a couple whenever you spy them at a yard sale. They don't have to match. A mixture of patterns and designs adds interest to your table; just focus on a color theme to help keep your tabletop coordinated.

Use your best every day. A conscientious gesture such as amassing a collection of silver-plated spoons for serving a crowd instead of forcing them to eat with plastic utensils sends a subtle message that your guests are important. Random pieces of silverware are a staple at most estate sales; matching sets are not necessary. The mixture of silver patterns will lend an eclectic mix to your setting. In the same vein, people are sometimes surprised when they get a cloth napkin at a party. Our family and friends are not disposable, and neither are we. A supply of mismatched silverware and sturdy cotton napkins will last for years.

A Buffet of Salvage

Serving buffet style is easiest for you and tends to result in a more relaxed atmosphere, with people eating whenever they want. A mix of dishes and serving pieces will work together as long as you establish a common theme or color.

First, cover your table with a tablecloth—or two or three! White linen tablecloths are easy to find at yard sales and thrift stores. They may have stains or holes in them, and nobody wants to iron these monstrosities any more. But if you wash them and immediately take them out of the dryer to fold them, they will have that chic tousled, wrinkled look. Layer the tablecloths over the surface, covering holes and stains in one cloth with another. Finish off your tabletop with a final flourish of old sheet music, vintage wallpaper, tattered maps—fit the theme to match your event. This layered technique also enables you to use whatever table you need for your buffet. A weather-stained patio table or a distressed folding table can stand in for a formal buffet, and no one will know the difference with such a beautiful cover to disguise its true identity.

Many of our favorite serving pieces and dining decor were rescued from the trash bin—cleaned up and reinvented, of course! As Lisa has already said, often the best use for a castoff can be found by turning it upside down. The rich patina of one rusted serving stand, an inverted farm pulley, was acquired after hanging for many years inside a barn. The round pulleys are now sturdy bottom feet, and a silver-plated fluted tray fits perfectly in the rimmed top to hold either a stack of plates or a selection of rolls.

Spare parts from broken or worn-out machinery make ideal trivets, as does anything that is flat, level,

More Party Favor Ideas

- Rubber-stamp a **paper envelope** with a favorite quote and place a small deck of playing cards inside.
- Adorn a paper envelope with rubber stamping and fill with lavender buds for an instant **sachet.**
- Waxed or glassine paper bags can contain a package of **flower or vegetable seeds.** Fold the top over, punch two holes in the top, and secure it closed with a piece of ribbon, twine, or a small section of pipe cleaner slipped in and out of the holes. If you're sharing the seeds from your favorite poppies, all the better! (Give the bag an extra fold or two to close it securely.)
- Your book club and everyone else will love extra **bookplates** slipped into these translucent bags as well.

An upside-down farm pulley and a variety of textures and finishes make a festive buffet in the Salvage Studio style.

---

and stable. (If the bottom surface is rough, add a piece of cork or felt, cut to size, to keep it from scratching the tabletop.) I particularly like a wooden disc we removed from a broken spinning wheel; as a trivet, it adds texture and warm color to my table.

A rusted metal rack holds a charming trio of glass bowls, perfect for condiments or antipasto, that fit into wire openings that once held canning jars. The rack now holds the bowls in place and provides a handle if the server needs to be moved. Glass shades and globes from large ceiling light fixtures make beautiful buffet pieces when their electrical fixtures are no longer of use. You can often locate a silver-plated casserole holder (usually missing its dish insert) and rest a large glass light dome on top. The hole in the center of the shade, where it attached to the light fixture, doesn't hamper its use as a serving dish for bread, rolls, grapes, or apples.

As described in the Serving Pedestals project, any number of combinations are possible for making Salvage Studio pedestals. Using a variety of pedestals on your buffet table adds immediate interest and height and allows you additional serving space so you're not confined to just the table surface. For example, you can attach a smaller glass light shade to a wooden candle base. Spray-paint the candle base a creamy white to match the shade, then attach the shade to the base with a wood screw and a small rubber gasket to cushion the screw against the glass. A fine selection of cheese or fruit can now be served from this wood and glass pedestal. You can also attach wire handles to smaller discarded glass lamp covers and hang them from a fireplace tool holder. A stunning centerpiece on the buffet table, the glass containers can hold flatware, napkins, flowers, candles, or even breadsticks. (See the Fireplace Tool-Holder Caddy project.)

Brass lamps, often not in working order, are a common find at thrift stores. Removing the wiring, swapping out the harp for a coaster or shallow dish, and then adding quirky shapes for embellishment gives you a tabletop candlestick to cast a warm glow. (See the Lamp Candleholder project.) Cherished photos, photocopied and inserted into plain glass canning jars set atop silver-plated glass coasters, are a stylish way to honor special party guests.

Inside or Outside, Junk It Up

Whether inside or out, the simplest of containers is all you need to set your table and serve your guests. Old enamelware containers in various shapes and sizes are

A wire glass caddy, with tin-can replacement inserts, holds silverware and napkins for outdoor dining.

Party Reflections and Traditions

Always serving Aunt Edna's apple pie at Thanksgiving or making salsa every summer with the first tomatoes from the garden is how food traditions are born. Years after all her children were grown, my mother continued to receive frantic phone calls from us, wanting her recipe for turkey stuffing or fudge brownie cake. She finally copied all of our childhood favorites and put them into a hand-bound notebook for each of us, the cover made from a scrap of fabric from one of her favorite dresses. To this day, it is one of my most treasured collections.

Make a conscious effort to begin such traditions of your own. Write down the details of a successful party or favorite menu and then repeat your efforts the following year. It will bring joy to the table for you, your family, and your guests.

ideal for outdoor buffets, since they are unbreakable. One of Beth's favorite outdoor serving dishes is her chip and dip holder made from a metal Christmas-tree stand. Simply remove the legs from the red basin. There is usually a center prong for inserting the tree trunk. Cover this prong with an inverted dish and stack another smaller bowl on top to hold the condiment. Encircle this center bowl with chips, and you have stylish yet simple appetizers.

Wire drinking-glass caddies from the 1950s are often tossed in the trash after the glasses are broken. But we've found that tin cans (our ubiquitous go-to container) fit

Simple Gifting Ideas

Having small gifts on hand is a real time-saver and stress reducer. It can be a challenge just to get out the door to a party or event with your teeth brushed, pot-luck dish in hand, and a little something for the host. Find an available small shelf or a well-labeled box to hold a variety of gifting items. I think of my area as a little gift pantry. This stash is also perfect for last-minute thank-you gifts.

Food gifts are universal—they are enjoyed by men and women, young and old. Some items, like jars of honey and boxes of tea, are shelf stable. If you run across a good buy on something yummy, buy an extra one as a future gift, and when the time comes, present it with a bit of flair. Say you find a tasty bottle of fruit syrup: tie a **small ceramic or glass pitcher,** culled from a thrift store, to the syrup bottle, using a pretty ribbon. Instead of the traditional bottle of wine, give your hostess a lovely blue-colored bottle of mineral water with a **stray crystal goblet** attached to its neck with wired ribbon. A food gift sure to score you billions of good guest points would be a jar of your homemade freezer jam or whatever specialty you might recently have made. Add a **butter knife**

or **small spreader** to the jam or a **cocktail fork** to your pickles.

You can gain a surplus of gifts by making extra items when you are crafting. If you are a card maker, you know that the majority of your project time is spent gathering the supplies. As long as you are set up, spend a few more moments to make extra cards. Wrap a **set of four handmade cards** with a piece of twine or enclose them in a waxed paper bag, sealed with a sticker. They're easy to store and a thoughtful treasure for the lucky recipient.

As we mentioned earlier, **china saucers** abound at garage and estate sales. The teacup bit the dust ages ago, but the saucer lasts forever, and with that little depression in the middle, it makes the perfect soap dish. Secure a bar of soap to the dish with a piece of ribbon, tucking in a sprig of lavender or other green-ery from your garden. A large **scallop shell** works as a dandy soap dish too. Place the soap on a bed of shredded sheet music to fill out the shell. Your every-day paper shredder transforms common papers into useful and attractive packaging material; atlas and dictionary pages have good graphics.

in as a great substitute. Napkins, silverware, and even flowers can fill the cans, and the caddy easily transports from kitchen to patio.

To add a touch of greenery to your outdoor dining table, insert fresh herbs into empty olive oil cans, which often feature vintage-looking labels. The green herbs

complement the graphics of the can and infuse your event with an informal air.

Foraged Favors

At the Studio, we believe that the smallest gesture resounds with the loudest response. Bringing a small but thoughtful gift to your host conveys your appreciation for him or her and your pleasure in sharing the food and festivities. Although a bouquet of flowers is standard practice and always lovely, finding a vase and arranging the flowers while prepping food or greeting other guests can be inconvenient for the host. Why not offer instead something that he or she can enjoy later?

———

Plant markers in a decorated tin can are a simple but charming hostess gift.

Food items or candles have universal appeal. A sliver of decadent chocolate or a sip of exotic white tea are small indulgences when relaxing after the guests are gone. An ordinary tin can, covered in decorative paper and given a silk ribbon handle, makes a sublime gift container for such items.

A Salvage Studio staple is a well-chosen vintage book wrapped as a prized hostess gift. After selecting a favorite volume, such as *Pride and Prejudice,* or an interesting topic, such as a horticultural manual for the

gardening enthusiast, just add a length of ribbon and a glittery ornament. A retro men's tie, wrapped twice around a packet of stationery, is effortless yet chic.

Since the days of childhood birthday parties and nut cups filled with treats, everyone loves a party favor. Giving out guest favors is one more extension of your hospitality. One simple solution is to have favors that double as place cards. A waxed paper sandwich bag lined with a sheet of colored tissue paper, filled with mints, and tied up with a name tag and a piece of twine or ribbon can be set on each dinner plate.

It's also nice to hand out favors as guests take their leave. I like to place wrapped candles in an opened antique tackle box located near the door. I melt the remains of used candle ends, then pour the hot wax into old jelly jars with a string wick. Easy but thoughtful is the meaning to convey.

Fireplace Tool-Holder Caddy

A versatile serving piece is born from a fireplace tool holder and cast-off glass shades from ceiling light fixtures, suitable for holding silverware, flowers, or candles. U-shaped fireplace tool holders, or those shaped like a wheel spoke, are easy to design with and easy to find. Make sure your glass shades have a lipped rim; you can choose a variety of shapes or use one shape for all. They should be different sizes but nothing too gigantic, or they will not nestle well with one another.

Materials:
- Fireplace tool holder
- 3 or 5 glass ceiling shades or domes from ceiling light fixtures
- 10 yards of 20-gauge wire
- 9 to 15 chandelier crystals or beads for embellishing (3 per lamp piece; optional)

Tools:
- Wire cutters
- Round-nose pliers

1. Remove any sooty residue from the tool holder. The holder can be painted, but I prefer the natural metal finish.
2. Each lamp will hang at a different height from the holder. As a rule, the bigger glass pieces work better at the lower heights. Since you can't hold all five pieces in the air at once to do a dry run, use your imagination and just get started. Wire is cheap, so it's easy to change your mind after you get going.
3. Start with the piece that will hang the lowest. Mea-

Discarded glass lamp globes are used as silverware caddies and embellished with wire and crystals.

sure enough wire to go around the neck of the lamp piece plus 6 inches for closing it with a decorative end, plus the length you want it to hang, plus another 6 inches to finish it closed at the top—about 36 inches in all. When in doubt, use more wire rather than less. Cut two pieces this length.

4. Circle the top of the glass shade with your wire, overlapping the ends, with one end 6 inches long and the other end what is left. Twist the wire together three times, securing it to the lamp piece as snugly as possible. With a pair of round-nose pliers, make little loops, starting at the end of the 6-inch piece, one after another, to form a decorative design. With your remaining long length, you can form three little loops spaced out along the length of your wire.

5. Repeat this procedure with the other piece of wire on the same glass lamp piece, with your overlapping closure directly opposite the first one.

6. Holding the two loose wires closed together with your hand, place it on the tool holder to make sure the shade will hang where you wanted it to. Adjust the length as needed before you twist the wires closed. The wire tails can be 6 inches or so long. Trim the extra wire length off. Make a decorative loop finish with the ends, as you did at the neck closure.

7. For each remaining glass shade, repeat the wire hanging instructions while staggering the lengths of the wire so each glass shade is at a different height.

8. Feel free to add crystal chandelier drops or beads to the wire loops for more pizzazz.

This Fireplace Tool-Holder Ccddy holds silverware at the buffet table but could also hold napkins or flowers.

Lamp Candleholder

A broken table lamp with some orphaned lamp parts, wire, and bits and bobs becomes a terrific candleholder for inside or out.

Materials:

- Brass metal table lamp
- Metal lamp spacers as needed
- Flat, bowl-shaped metal lamp part, wide enough to suspend decorative metal pieces from, and with a hole in the middle big enough to slip over the metal inside rod of the lamp (in its former life, this piece probably held or supported the glass lamp shade)
- Lamp nut and washer
- 3 yards of 20-gauge wire
- 5 to 10 decorative metal bits and bobs, such as attractive hinges, keyhole plates, faucet handles, locker key numbers, skeleton keys, and window locks
- 6- to 12-inch pillar candle

Tools:

- Wire cutters
- Metal hole punch or nail
- Hammer, if punching holes using a nail
- Round-nose pliers

1. Disassemble the lamp by cutting the cord off at the lamp base, using wire cutters. Remove the socket by unscrewing it and/or popping it out of the socket base. Remove the harp holder, if there is one, where it attaches underneath the socket.

2. Unfortunately, you usually can't just place the orphaned lamp piece that is going to hold your candle on the exposed threaded rod and be done with it. The socket space needs a little filling in. This is where your miscellaneous lamp parts are quite handy. Most lamp parts marry well with each other. Slip some spacers over the rod to fill in the space. You want to have about ¼ inch of exposed rod left showing.

3. Before you place the bowl-shaped lamp piece that will hold your candle over the rod, use a metal hole punch to make three or five holes evenly spaced around the edge of the piece to suspend your decorations from. If you don't have a metal hole punch, a nail and hammer will usually work. (If you find a piece with a filigree edge, your wire will attach to the openwork, and no holes will be needed.) Once the holes are made, slip this piece over the rod, attach a washer and nut, and tighten it together.

4. To create your hanging decorations, cut pieces of

Whimsical metal ephemera, such as old locker numbers and garden faucets, decorate this Lamp Candleholder.

wire 12 to 18 inches in length, depending on how ornate you want the wire to be. Slip a piece of wire through one of the decorations, center it, and twist the wire closed two times, near the decoration. Using a pair of round-nose pliers, start at the end of each piece of wire and bend little loops, one after another, to make flourishes. For more complex decorations, you can create several decorations and attach them to one another. An asymmetrical balance looks interesting. Use short lengths of wire, 6 inches or so, to connect one piece to another and to the previously made holes in the candleholder.

5. To get your candle to sit flat in your candleholder, you will have to carve a tiny opening inside the base of the candle to make room for the protruding portion of the threaded rod and the nut. This will also anchor your candle more securely to the candleholder.

Serving Pedestals

Pedestals add a touch of elegance and élan to your buffet table. Marrying two elements together makes a practical yet stylish serving solution, and the possibilities are endless. Our four favorite combinations are these:

- Glass with glass
- Glass with silver plate
- Silver plate with silver plate
- Silver plate with wood

Silver Plate with Wood Pedestal

Many candlesticks from the 1960s and '70s were chunky wooden designs, often overvarnished. They seem to multiply at the thrift stores, since they now look so dated. Reworking them into these pedestals gives them a fresh new look.

Materials:

- Sturdy wooden candlestick
- Black spray paint
- Round silver-plated tray
- Wood glue or epoxy
- One No.8 wood screw
- Cork or self-adhesive felt, approximately 6 inches square (optional)

Tools:

- 60-grit sandpaper
- Ruler
- Pencil
- Permanent marking pen
- Center punch or nail
- Hammer
- Power drill with drill bit to match the screw
- Safety goggles
- Screwdriver to match the head of the screw

1. Sand the candlestick to abrade any varnish and smooth the rough edges; this will make it easier for the paint to adhere.

2. Spray several light coats of black paint onto the candlestick. It is better to spray several light coats instead of one or two heavy coats, because the resulting finish will be even and less likely to drip. Allow 2 to 3 hours between coats. After you have finished painting, allow the candlestick to dry completely, at least 24 hours.

3. Find the center of the silver-plated tray by drawing two lines across the diameter, with a ruler and pencil. Mark a dot where the lines intersect, using a permanent marking pen. With a hammer and center punch or nail, make a pilot hole for drilling. Use the drill to make a hole equal in diameter to the diameter of the screw you are using. Wear safety goggles when drilling. See "Drilling Silver Plate" in the Look chapter for more information.

4. Determine which end of your painted candlestick will be the top. Sometimes the bottom is sturdier than the top; if so, turning it upside down and attaching the tray to this surface will give you a better weighted

pedestal. Mark the center of the candlestick and drill a pilot hole for the screw.

5. Dab a small amount of glue or epoxy onto the bottom of the tray and the top of the candlestick where you will be attaching the tray. Align the hole in the center of the tray with the hole in the center of the candlestick and attach them together, using a wood screw.

6. Depending upon how rough the bottom of your candlestick is, you may want to adhere a piece of cork or black felt to it to protect your tabletop.

Silver Plate and Glass Pedestals

The pedestals made using all silver plate, all glass, or a combination of silver plate and glass are very easy to assemble. The magic ingredient is a strong and simple-to-use glue. Our favorite is Amazing Goop's Lawn & Garden Formula, found at craft stores and home improvement centers. It is UV resistant, so your creations can survive outside and inside your home. You don't have to mix it, and it rubs off of your fingers—eventually!

Materials:

Silver plate:

- Goblet with a flared drinking cup and sturdy stem and foot for your base
- Tray, shallow bowl, plate, or platter for your main surface
- Various other pieces, such as candlesticks, bowls, and coasters

_____

Using a mix of silver plate and glass, these elegant Serving Pedestals are a stylish look for entertaining.

Recipe: Dried Apple Pie

Serves:

from Household Discoveries 1908

Soak apples, put in brown earthen pot, cover with water, cover the pot & bake four to five hours, sweeten with sugar or molasses the last half hour, mash well with a spoon, when thoroughly cooked, flavor with lemon juice & a little butter. The pie can be baked between two crust, or bands of paste can be placed over the top.

Glass:

- Goblet with a strong drinking cup and sturdy stem for your base
- Plates, bowls, candlesticks, teacups, and sugar or creamer pieces for the top and/or as layers in between

(Left) A silver-plated casserole holder has long ago lost its original insert, but a re-purposed glass cover fits perfectly and makes a fine fruit bowl. (Below) Vintage plates add a splash of color to the salvage-style cake pedestal, made from a silver-plated tray attached to a painted pedestal.

Tools:

- Clear, waterproof, UV-resistant glue, such as Amazing Goop's Lawn & Garden Formula
- Sharp craft knife, such as an X-Acto knife

1. Carefully do a dry run, stacking the pieces together to see whether they balance and look pleasing.
2. Figure out where the two pieces make contact, and apply the glue to each contact point.
3. After the two pieces are attached, let gravity help you. You want the glue to flow toward your point of contact, which might mean turning the piece upside down as it dries.
4. When the glue has set, use a sharp craft knife to trim away any excess glue that has oozed out.
5. Let your piece dry for several days to let the glue cure before you use it.

create

At the Salvage Studio, we encourage our customers to designate a place or haven in their own home to create. Think of it as your nest, with your creative supplies and salvaged loot close at hand. If it has a door to offer more privacy, quiet, and contemplative possibilities, you have it made in the hay. This space might be a closet or cupboard or table in the basement for starters. The point is to carve out a space in which you can feel comfortable and be creative.

Creative Space

I need solitude to create. No background music for me. The creative process can be chaotic enough without any additional distractions. For other people I know, however, their iPods jump-start an inspiration as much as any other art supplies do. Some practical, physical considerations for a crafting space include good lighting. Natural light is best but not always available; be grateful for that basement window! Besides any overhead lighting, supplement your space with task lighting. Just recently I finally coughed up the money for a nice full-spectrum floor lamp with a flexible neck. I no longer have to wonder if that button I'm gluing is navy blue or black.

A sturdy work table with as much surface room as your space will permit is next. I mainly sit while I cre-

Supplies at your fingertips: wooden rulers in a glass vase, rolls of tickets, ribbons galore.

ate (be sure to choose a comfortable chair!), so I've been happy with an affordable banquet table from the warehouse store. Of course, one with a snappy surface, like one of Amy's collaged tabletops, would be ideal. (Don't use a table that is too nice, however. I had a friend build a workbench for me incorporating a butcher-block top I found. He created a masterpiece anybody would be proud to have as their dining room table. I keep a portion of it covered with a towel to protect it while I work. Not ideal!) Amy prefers to stand while she creates, so her favorite work surface is higher.

When it comes to flooring, we generally simply accept what is there. Keep in mind, however, that the easier it is to clean up, the better. I work in a guest bedroom with wall-to-wall carpeting, so any painting projects get removed to the laundry room. But I figure the exercise of traveling between the two rooms is good for me, and the laundry-room windows open wide for ventilation, another important consideration if you are painting or using strong glues and resins.

Ready, Set, Go!

For me, the more organized I am, the more creative I can be. When I sit down to make something, I want to see at once all the possible materials I can use. If a project needs some ribbon, for example, Lisa's ribbon frame is ideal (see the Picture-Frame Ribbon Hanger project). The choices can be arranged by color or texture or however your brain works. Immediately you

Wow—how many ideas can you spot in this photo? A guest bedroom does double duty as an organized and attractive paradise for creating. It is a dream to work in a space where you can see and access your supplies in such style.

can see the ribbon array and pull off what you need.

Single pieces of ribbon can be trickier to keep tidy but are just as valuable to crafting as whole spools. A wall organizer made from a rake can hold these single strands as easily as it holds your necklaces (see the Garden-Rake Wall Holder project). I admit I have a thing for ribbon, and I even designate friends and family as "ribbon worthy." So I have a stash of single pieces of ribbon too vast for the rake holder. Instead I put each color in an open plastic bag, then place the bags side by side in a clear plastic box. The only digging I have to do is within each bag, and usually I can see what I am aiming for through the clear plastic.

A wooden hanger can hold your favorite spools of ribbon or twine too. Choose a wooden pants hanger with an adjustable bottom piece that opens and closes. Usually a metal bar runs parallel to this wooden piece. With a heavy-duty pair of wire cutters, clip the metal bar on the side where the wooden bar attaches. Slip your favorite spools over both bars and hang your hanger somewhere convenient.

We love clear compact-disc cases for containing and separating our small pieces of ephemera such as tickets, fortunes from cookies, and dried and pressed flowers. Each category gets its own case. You can label and embellish your cases as Amy has or leave them clear and let the contents speak for themselves. I hung a wall-mounted CD holder in my home studio and now have easy access to a large stack of cases. Many units will fit in small, odd sections of your wall space, which frees up more of the valuable real estate known as your work table.

Yet another way to use tin cans—and to organize your creative materials—is to fashion them into a portable caddy. Use a large No.10 can (the size used in restaurants) as your center, and attach small 15-ounce cans around its rim. A hammer and nail are low-tech ways to create all the holes you need for affixing the small cans to the big one, as well as a couple more holes

---

How to Renew a Tired Bulletin Board

1. Select a framed corkboard, making sure the cork itself is still in good shape.

2. Figure out a hanger, such as two ½-inch screws attached to the back side of the frame, in the top center, about 2 inches apart, with a 6-inch piece of (20 gauge) wire wrapped around each screw.

3. Spray-paint the entire thing, frame and cork, one color. If the frame is in good shape and you want to retain the natural wood color, cover the frame portion with masking tape. My personal preference is for a united background, although it really doesn't matter because any well-loved idea board is going to have every inch covered.

4. Figure out a simple grid (vertical, horizontal, and/or diagonal lines) on which to lay out your ribbons; cut lengths of ribbon to fit the width or length of your board within the frame, depending on your grid.

5. Attach the ribbons in the center of each grid intersection with upholstery tacks or furniture nails. (These are like long thumbtacks with decorative heads.)

---

for your handle. A medium 20-gauge wire is sturdy enough for attaching each can individually and for making a handle for carrying.

We use metal toolboxes a lot. They come in all sizes, shapes, and colors. I like the ones that have a removable tray as well as the ones that have two shelves that fold out. When closed, toolboxes have handles and are highly portable for crafting on the go. I could go on and on about my love for toolboxes! (Try to avoid the ones with oily, globby residue; it will eventually come off with a gentle cleanser and plenty of scrubbing, but inevitably some of that oil gets on a project.) I do lots of projects with broken lamps. The beauty of lamp pieces is that the parts mix and match with one another. A glass shade for a ceiling light fixture marries a floor lamp, and you have a birdbath. Several lamps mix together, and you have a candelabra. As I dissect a lamp, each part gets put with similar pieces in a cubby in my toolbox.

We've talked about storing your treasures for art in clear canning jars or other large jars. I keep six open jars in a salvaged metal refrigerator drawer (1950s era) close to my work table. With no lid to deal with, I can add and remove objects lickety-split. The creative process loves lickety-split. In the middle of a project, it is no fun at all to have to stop and start digging for a certain component.

Brilliant Ideas

Part of the creative process for me is collecting my thoughts and remembering them. We've all been there—you have a brilliant idea one night, only to forget it by the next day. Maybe the idea was triggered by a picture in a magazine, a card you received, or a gorgeous leaf you found while walking. Round these pieces of eye candy up and put them on an idea board. Corkboards, often available on the secondhand circuit, can be refurbished to add a little zip to your creative space, as well as contain all your good ideas.

A second way to capture your ideas is to keep a blank notebook handy. Jot down your idea with enough description to actually know what you meant a day later. Maybe you are good at drawing and can sketch out what

Corral canning jars of ephemera in an old enamel refrigerator drawer.

you envision. Record your creative thoughts in any way that works for you.

Another fun way to display your ideas—or handmade cards or small artworks—is on a memo holder made of garden fencing, designed by Amy. It is freestanding and lovely to look at all by itself. Attach favorite ideas with wooden clothespins or other clips; they can easily be updated and changed (see the Garden-Fencing Memo Holder project).

Creative Support

If you find you are a bit hesitant to start creating on your own, or you've started and now feel as though you are stuck in a rut, I encourage you to sign up for a class. It's an effective way to start whacking away at your creative resistance. As Lisa describes in the Look chapter, a group setting can nudge you into new territory. I'm a firm believer in the notion that the more you share your ideas, the more you will receive. We see this principle come to life week after week at Studio workshops. One idea turns into a gazillion. The actual hands-on project is just one small element. Resources and favorite books are discussed, while recommendations for favorite glues and blogs and other hot tips are passed from one end of the table to the other.

Crafting "girl groups," much like the ubiquitous book club, have become more common in recent years. Organize your own group of like-minded friends to meet on a regular basis to do art or some other creative endeavor together. Lisa and I are fortunate to belong to a group, Women of the Arts, whose members take turns hosting monthly "art days," in which we all work on one project. Sometimes the hostess selects and provides materials for the project; sometimes we decide on a project ahead of time and each bring our own supplies. Either way, there is always a huge amount of sharing—supplies, tools, and laughs. People who have taken a class and learned a new technique will teach everyone else what they have learned. I found a darn cute little suitcase at a thrift store, embellished the top, and now keep extra supplies and tools inside it as my traveling toolbox for these art days.

Then there is the concept of crafting play dates—less frequent and less structured, but still an important source of creative support. As much as I like to visit with someone, drink coffee, or eat lunch, I'd rather be making something while I'm there! A friend and I might take a class together to learn something new. Or we might get together in one of our homes for a show-and-tell of our latest creations. Sometimes a little field trip evolves into a car full of women headed out for creative exploration.

On top of such friendly and intimate possibilities as crafting groups and play dates is the more "rigorous" world of swaps and trades. These involve deadlines and might include people you don't know or even professional artists. As much as the stipulation of "finishing a project by a given date" can be stressful, it's also sort of handy. I don't think I'm the only one who starts more projects than I can finish, and an organized swap or trade forces me to get the job done! We recently held our first charm swap at the Studio. Twenty-five people brought 25 jewelry charms to trade with everyone else. It was magical! I came up with one charm idea and made 24 more charms very similar to the first. In return, I received 24 imaginative, lovely, whimsical, and unique pieces. The group even decided to repeat this little slice of artistic heaven in six months. If it's hard for you to find a group of fel-

low crafters in your area, you will be overwhelmed with all the swap choices on the Internet. There are Yahoo groups galore as well as dedicated sites. Lisa and I have both participated in some of these events.

A popular workshop we cooked up at the Studio is based on a similar approach: I give each participant a metal expansion bracelet, which resembles a watchband, with 80-plus spots to attach broken jewelry and other flotsam. Although I provide kits for everyone, with plenty of found objects to fill their bracelets, I also encourage them to personalize their project with their own special relics. Each bracelet takes on its own distinct personality. Jewelry made from found objects has a very strong appeal for fans of salvage. Each piece tells a story and is one of a kind. It's genuine. It's personal. We recognize the bracelet or necklace components as everyday objects, but once assembled, the piece transcends these to become art (see the Found-Objects Bracelet project).

I sometimes joke that Earth is not my planet. I figure I was in a spaceship, fiddling around with the doors, fell out, and landed here. I avoid the mall as much as possible. Instead, I like to find things. (Though I do like to shop at thrift stores, church rummage sales, and estate sales.) I like to create things from what I find and share those ideas. Week after week, I meet so many people who totally get what we do at the Studio. Some are surprised that "junk" can be so beautiful and fun and useful. Some enter our studio, realize that this is what they've been looking for, and express relief and gratitude. And we are equally grateful that this creative community of ours is growing.

We want people to see differently. If you are inspired by the meaningfulness and usefulness of everyday objects, you will feel motivated to create more meaning, function, and beauty in your daily life.

Out of Sight, Out of Mind

If you are able to see your supplies and treasures, you are more likely to use them. If you have to move this box and that one to get to the bottom one, it's likely you won't be "needing" stuff in that bottom box as often. And let's face it, we all have stacks of boxes. Those containing your favorite supplies will gravitate to the top. Until you can find the time to evaluate what items aren't getting used, keep those favorites on top. But every so often, look in those bottom boxes too. You might realize that your tastes have changed and it's time to empty that box and share the contents with other artists or crafting friends. We have a free box at the Studio by our front door. The contents rarely linger. When our artist trading-card group meets monthly, there is usually some sharing and transferring of supplies within the group. Anything that is not adopted is given to one of our favorite local charities. (You can also offer your extra art supplies to any schoolteachers or child-care providers in your area.)

I like to use a vintage typewriter I found at an estate sale. When I want to add a custom phrase to a paper arts project, I can do so quickly—no computer to turn on or file to find. I keep it on an old typing table adjacent to my work table; if I had the typewriter put away in its case somewhere, that little extra effort to extract it would make me think twice about using it.

Picture-Frame Ribbon Hanger

Several years ago my neighbor Samantha had a big, gaudy wooden picture frame next to her garbage can on trash day. Of course I had to knock on the door and ask if I could have it. This became the first ribbon hanger, and I still have and use it to this day. The basic idea is to make a shallow box that will hold adjustable wooden dowels on which your spools of ribbon will hang.

Materials:

- Large, beefy wooden picture frame, 2 by 3 feet or larger
- Primed 1-by-4 boards
- 1⅛-inch finishing nails or ¾-inch No.8 wood screws
- 2 cans satin-finish spray paint
- 2 eye hooks
- 2 feet of picture wire
- Wall anchor for hanging frame on wall
- 4 wooden dowels, ⅜ inch in diameter

Tools:

- Table saw, circular saw, or jigsaw
- Drill press or hand-held power drill
- ³⁄₁₆-inch and ½-inch drill bits
- Safety goggles

- Hammer or screwdriver (depending on whether you're using nails or screws)
- Medium-grit sandpaper

1. Before you start, determine where the thickest part of the frame is. This is where you will attach the wooden box you make. Size the box appropriately. For example, if the hole in the frame is 8 by 10 inches, the inside of the box needs to be that size. If the thickness of the 1-by-4 is ¾ inch, you would cut two 8-inch-long pieces (one for the top and one for the bottom of the box) and two 11½-inch-long pieces (10 inches plus the thickness of the top and bottom boards). The two side pieces will screw or nail into the top and bottom pieces from the sides.

2. Cut top, bottom, and side pieces of primed 1-by-4 wood based on the size of your frame. (Wear safety goggles when using a power saw or drill.)

3. Take the two sides and clamp them together or nail them together temporarily so you can drill holes through them both at the same time. That way,

Hoarding ribbons? All can be displayed and ready to use in an instant.

when the box is assembled, the holes on both sides line up nicely. Drill holes slightly larger than the dowels you are going to hang the ribbon spools on (½ inch for ⅜-inch dowels). A 1-inch spacing of the holes works well and allows for maximum adjustability of the dowels. Make sure the holes are fairly close to the inside edge of the box where the frame will be attached but far enough away that the dowels will clear the frame itself.

4. Drill pilot holes in the wood with a ³⁄₁₆-inch drill bit. Put the box together with screws or nails.

5. Attach the box to the picture frame. Either nails or screws will do the job, but you must be very careful not to nail or screw through the front of the picture frame. I know, because I've done it. To be on the safe side, you can toenail the box to the frame, using nails or screws driven in at an angle to fasten it to the frame. (Toenailing is a carpentry term for joining two pieces of wood by driving in nails at an angle. It works great for hard-to-reach areas or ones where you want a good connection but don't have a lot of wood to work with.) Drill a pilot hole straight into the wood on the box, gradually increasing the angle until you end up with a hole that runs through the piece at about a 45-degree angle. Now the nail or screw has a clear path thorough the box and into the picture frame and has less chance of going off in the wrong direction.

6. After the box is attached to the frame, you can paint. Always paint in a well-ventilated area, preferably outside. I use a satin-finish spray paint for ease; it goes into all the little cracks and holes. I always paint the back first and let it dry thoroughly according to the directions on the paint can. Then I paint the front. Sometimes the best old frames have a fabric strip on the front of the frame; I paint right over it.

7. Attach the two eye hooks to the back and add picture wire. You will need a sturdy screw or nail in your wall to hang the ribbon hanger. I suggest using a wall anchor, readily available at hardware stores.

8. Using a table saw, circular saw, or jigsaw, cut the dowels to fit through the holes, adding 1 inch on either side so they extend out from the sides of the box. Lightly sand the ends, if needed, with medium-grit sandpaper. There's no need to paint the dowels. Place the dowels through the holes, adding your ribbon spools as you go.

Garden-Rake Wall Holder

A common garden rake with a broken handle easily transforms into a handy and decorative wall organizer. The fan-shaped metal variety works best; it's OK if it's missing a tine or two. Rakes are easy to find at garage sales. Note: It is against our junk ethics to cut up a perfectly good rake for this project!

Materials:

- Metal garden rake
- About 24 inches of 18- or 20-gauge wire

Tools:

- Saw (I like to use a jigsaw, but a common wood saw is fine)
- Safety goggles
- Medium-grit sandpaper, such as 120
- Section of wooden dowel about 1 inch in diameter and 6 to 12 inches in length
- Rubber mallet (optional)
- Needle-nose pliers
- Wire cutters

This holder looks great empty or filled. At the Studio, it holds necklaces for sale. At home, I have one by the front door for hats and scarves.

1. Cut off the wooden handle as close to the metal rake as possible. I find my jigsaw makes quick work of this and does a fine job. If you have a manual wood saw, that will work well also. Wear safety goggles when using a power saw.

2. Sand the wood stub smooth.

3. Lay the rake on a flat surface with the tines curling under. Bend every other tine upward, toward the sky, forming a 90-degree angle, using a section of wooden dowel (maybe the wooden handle you just sawed off) to brace the lower portion of the tine where you are bending it. If you just pull the tine upward with nothing supporting its base, it may snap off. (Voice of experience talking here.)

4. To have your rake lie flush against the wall for hanging, flatten the curling ends of the tines that are still straight. You can whack them flatter with a rubber mallet or place the rake on your garage floor, with the remaining unbent tines curling under, and stand on the curly part.

5. To hang your rake, make a hanger from the piece of wire. Form a 1-inch circle of wire in the middle and twist it closed with three twists. Find the middle of the back of your rake and lay the wire circle flat against the rake. Extend each end of the wire out and around the two adjoining tines on either side of the circle, going over and under the tines. Also wrap each wire end around a stationary part of the rake, such as the horizontal metal piece that is attached to the tines. Rejoin the ends with several twists and cut off any excess wire.

Found-Objects Bracelet

Everyday bits and pieces gathered together transform into a stunning bracelet. I designed my bracelet using mainly metals, from a St. Christopher medal given to me by my son to my girl-of-the-month high school pin, with a few glass objects. Mixing beads from one color family with the found objects creates an entirely distinctive look for each bracelet. I display my bracelet on the neck of a clear, clean chili sauce bottle. I can't tell you how happy this piece of jewelry makes me feel; it's a keepsake.

From sentimental icons to rusty relics rescued from the bottom of the junk drawer—all are happy neighbors on this piece of jewelry.

Materials:

- 80+ found items, such as broken jewelry, small keys, sewing machine bobbins, buttons, beads, watch parts, washers, nuts, jacks, glass fuses, small tree lights, springs, links from chains, fishing lures, coins, religious medals, zipper pulls, tiny sections of rulers, pen nibs, tiny keyholes, rusty safety pins, and Scrabble letters

Wonderful charms from the first Salvage Studio charm swap adorn this necklace.

- 100+ sturdy jump rings, 6 mm
- 20+ jump rings, 8 mm
- Metal expansion/stretch bracelet with places to attach jump rings (found at craft or jewelry supply stores, these look like watchbands with loops attached)
- About 10 yards of 22-gauge wire (silver colored works well)

Tools:

- 2 pairs small needle-nose pliers (if you have jewelry tools, use flat-nose and chain-nose pliers)
- Multipurpose rotary tool with small ($\frac{3}{64}$-or $\frac{1}{16}$-inch) drill bit, small collet nuts to hold the extra-small bits, cutting disc, and sander attachment
- Center punch or small nail
- Hammer
- Locking pliers, such as Vise-Grips
- Safety goggles
- Metal hole punch, the more delicate the better
- Wire cutters
- Round-nose pliers
- Tin snips
- Sandpaper or metal file

1. Assemble all your possible found-object charms together. You'll want to balance out the placement of your largest objects. If you have multiples of larger items, you could lay them out in a pattern. Attach these large items first.
2. Most items can be secured to the bracelet with a jump ring. Use two pairs of pliers to partially open your jump rings. Hold the jump ring with one pair of pliers, with the opening facing upward. With the

second pair of pliers, grip the other side of the jump ring and swivel that side forward slightly. Still holding the jump ring with one pair of pliers, attach your found object, hook it onto the bracelet loop, and use the second pair of pliers again to close the jump ring. When possible, use the smaller 6 mm jump rings. The focus should be on the object, not on a large jump ring. But to attach bulkier objects, the larger 8 mm jump rings will work better.

3. Some items will need a hole added. If it is a wooden or plastic object, a multipurpose rotary tool will work best. Invest in a set of small drill bits, which requires the purchase of the small collet nuts to hold them. Most rotary tools come with a ⅛-inch drill bit, which is too large for this project. If you are drilling something like a Scrabble tile, first make a pilot hole with a center punch or small nail. This creates a small impression for your drill bit to enter. Place the tile in the jaws of a pair of locking pliers. Do not be tempted to hold the tile with your fingers! We love phone books for drilling surfaces, but old plastic or wooden cutting boards no longer suitable for kitchen use work equally well. Don your safety goggles. Set the drill at a medium speed and brace your elbow on your work surface close to your object for support. You'll know when the drill bit is all the way through the object because it will sound different. Gently remove the drill bit from the object. A bit will break every so often. They are somewhat delicate but, fortunately, not that expensive. It's part of the learning curve. Sometimes, when you are drilling plastic game tiles, some plastic will melt onto your bit. When it has cooled, it will chip off with a little picking.

4. To put a hole in a metal object for this project, we recommend a metal hole punch. The one mentioned in "Our Top 10 Tools" in the Look chapter—"Big Earl"—has a small bit that creates an attractive hole and is strong enough to go through a coin with a little muscle power. If you have jewelry tools, the common two-hole punch creates an even more delicate hole.

5. Sometimes a jump ring won't attach a wide or odd-shaped object. If there is a hole somewhere in the object, use a small section of wire, 4 to 6 inches or so, to create your own hanger. Insert the wire through the hole, twist the ends together three times at the base of the object, snip off one end of the wire close to the twist, and form a loop suitable for a jump ring to attach to with the other end of the wire. Snip off the excess.

6. If the object doesn't have a hole, like a small glass fuse or tree light, wrap it in a piece of wire. Start with a 12-inch section of wire and wrap it around the object in a free-form fashion, overlapping and securing the starting end of the wire. Work from bottom to top. Leave 2 inches to create your hanger. With a pair of round-nose pliers, form a small loop in the remaining wire about ⅛ inch above your object. Take the tail of the wire and wrap it three times just underneath the loop. Snip off any excess wire.

7. To cut a metal measuring tape into small sections, use a pair of tin snips. It's a Goldilocks situation: some snips are too big and some are too small. Use the sander attachment on your rotary tool or a piece of sandpaper or a metal file to smooth the edges.

8. Try your finished bracelet on and give it a couple of shakes. Any loose objects, usually due to jump rings that are not entirely closed, will tumble off. Reattach them and give those jump rings an extra squeeze.

Garden-Fencing Memo Holder

Old wire garden fencing and discarded scraps of molding marry to make a clever memo holder to keep track of creative ideas.

Materials:

- 2 to 4 sections of wire garden fencing—the type used as border edging (the sections are usually 12 to 16 inches long and about 18 inches high)
- Scrap piece of wooden molding, 2 inches longer than the length of your garden fencing and at least ⅜ inch thick
- Wood glue or your favorite epoxy

Tools:

- Lineman's pliers
- Sandpaper, if needed
- Paint or stain, if needed
- Pencil
- Wire cutters
- Hand-held power drill
- ¹⁄₁₆-inch drill bit
- Safety goggles
- Small rubber bumpers or self-adhesive cork (optional)

1. Begin by laying out your garden fencing. The fencing usually is divided into sections that easily connect to each other. Determine the length of your fencing and ensure that the wire sections lie flat, bending any bent sections back into alignment. Where sections of fencing connect, secure those connections. This is most readily accomplished by using pliers to smoosh adjoining wires together.

2. Prepare the molding for the base. Sand any rough edges. If the molding is unpainted, feel free to paint or stain it. Most recycled molding has been painted in a previous life and already has a fabulous finish. Determine the placement of the fencing by centering the fencing on the molding. Mark with a pencil where each of the bottom prongs of the fencing meet the molding. If the bottom prongs are not all the same length, even them out to a uniform length, using wire cutters.

3. At each location that you have marked, drill a hole through the molding with a ¹⁄₁₆-inch drill bit. Wear

This nifty organizer needs no installation—we love free-standing things. Plus, it is totally portable and can be put to work where needed.

safety goggles when drilling. The prongs of the fencing will fit snugly into these holes and hold the fencing upright.

4. Dab a small amount of glue or epoxy into each drilled hole and insert a fencing prong into each hole, flush with the underside of the molding.

5. Depending upon how rough the underside of your molding is, you may want to attach small rubber bumpers or a length of self-adhesive cork backing to protect your tabletop.

6. Your memo holder is now ready for use. You can either insert note cards and reminders between the wire sections or use wooden clothespins to attach your memos to the fencing stand.

LISA

reflect

The end of the day should be reserved for you and your family. We know how hectic your lives are; you don't need anyone to tell you! Personally, I don't answer the phone after 8 p.m., and all my friends and family know that. I have made a conscious decision to be done with the outside world and all its influences after that time. If I didn't, it would creep its way into the evening. And that is personal time, time to decompress and reflect.

Amy likes to have a private moment with her partner, Monty, when he comes home from work; it's their time to connect and talk about their separate days. Her sister Stacey lives in the house behind them, so later the two households get together to check in with each other before dinner. Amy fondly refers to this time of day as

Happy Hour. Having a set time to gather makes the routine an important daily priority.

Lighting Reflection

Candlelight softens everything in its sphere. The lighting of a candle has been an age-old ritual for centuries. Incorporate that act into your own ritual of winding down for the evening. Amy likes to have an unscented candle burning as she prepares the evening meal. Besides its beauty, a burning candle helps absorb the fumes from a cut onion

———

Create a winter wonderland on your mantle. A JOY sign and simple candle grouping will carry you well into January.

that make you cry. I use a beeswax candle my sister made for me as my onion candle. I keep it in my onion basket so it is easy to find when it's onion-chopping time.

Have dinner by candlelight to help the whole family transition from work, school, and chores into the cocoon of the home. It will make you and your family feel special. If you are lucky, voices will lower and better table manners may even appear! Dinnertime is an excellent way to connect with loved ones, when each person can share his or her reflections on the day.

One of my favorite ways to display candles is on candlestick holders made from rusty old gears. If you have access to a farm or a heavy-equipment repair shop, you can obtain some intriguing gears; look for ones with vestiges of the original tractor color on them (see the Metal-Gear Candlesticks project). For a more elegant appearance, you can stack glass plates, bowls, and cream and sugar bowls. Glue all the pieces together, and your candle will be nested in sparkling style. Display your candles in groups of three or five, and vary the heights of your candelabra for a more interesting look (see the Serving Pedestals project in the Entertain chapter).

My husband, Doug, and I break out of our workday routine by enjoying a beverage together in what Doug calls the Sunset Garden. When he first called it that, I thought it was because it was in the southwest corner of our garden and we could enjoy the sunset from it. But when I asked him, he said it was so beautiful that it belonged in *Sunset* magazine. We sit and relax by a small pond made from an old bathtub I salvaged from

A cozy corner is complete with comfy chair, candlelight, and a cup of tea. Old refrigerator coils hung on the wall add an interesting backdrop to framed prints.

Basic Bath-Salts Recipe

Lavender is an easy herb to find or grow, and it has been used for centuries for its relaxing properties.

¼ cup Epsom salts

2 tablespoons sea salt

1 tablespoon baking soda

1 tablespoon dried lavender

Mix everything together. Fill a muslin tea bag or tea-ball strainer with the mixture. Run bath water over it and enjoy.

---

the house across the street and enjoy the sound of the water fountain we created together from an old floor lamp. Doug and I work together as a team quite a bit. I will gather items that I know have potential and come up with ideas for them. Doug contributes engineering solutions. I found an old floor lamp at a garage sale; the wiring had been damaged, but that didn't bother me because the instant I saw it, I knew the lamp would make a great water fountain. I brought it home, Doug figured out the mechanics, and we have enjoyed our fountain ever since. We also created a fountain from a table lamp. To catch and hold the water, we set it in an old cast-iron wok on a bistro table base, and it graces the entry to our home (see the Table-Lamp Fountain project).

Bath time and candles can be the perfect combination for ending the day. Make your own candles by melting down candle stubs that you have on hand, or be on the lookout for candles in the free boxes at garage sales. Broken and half-burned candles are everywhere once you start looking. I melt mine in a tin can set in a saucepan of hot water on the stove. Watch closely. I bend the tin can so that it has a pour spout of sorts. Amy uses an old Crock-pot that is now reserved just for candle making. On the lowest setting, the heat is enough to melt wax but low enough to lessen the fire hazard. Jelly jars and old teacups work great as recycled candle forms. Place a wick in your new container. I tie the wick to an old chopstick, skewer, or pencil and place it over the cup so that the wick hangs down into the center of the container. Carefully pour the wax in and allow it to cool. Cut the wick off the chopstick.

Another element of any nighttime bath ritual is fragrance. Lavender has long been known for its relaxing properties. Place homemade bath salts in a tea-ball strainer and hook it over your faucet to infuse the ingredients into your bath water as your tub fills. You can also use a muslin tea bag, available at most tea shops and health food stores. Bath salts make a sweet and easy gift too. (See Basic Bath-Salts Recipe.)

Quiet Reflection

As you lie in bed at the end of the day, do a recap. Beth quietly reviews all the wonderful things that have happened to her that day. Amy talks to Monty about larger issues and what's happening in the world. It helps her appreciate what she has in her own life and reinforces for her how important it is to be involved in the world around us.

Create your own journal: Tattered old books or colorful game boards resurrected as journal covers can be inspirational in and of themselves. Spend some quiet time and jot down the highlights of your day. Did you accomplish a big goal? A small one? Did you hear a funny story? Did someone share a quote that resonated with you? Is there a good book you heard about that you would like to read? List the blessings. Write these thoughts down

to make it real. Start with just one a day; soon you will have more than you can imagine. Many books have been written about how and why to keep a journal, for a very good reason. It works to help you relax and reflect (see the Recycled Blank Journals project).

Sometimes you don't have the luxury of a full and satisfying nighttime ritual. And, of course, you can pause to reflect throughout the day. In fact, we highly recommend it. Beth and I both leave the radios off in our cars while we drive. Beth uses her time to send mental wishes of good health to those she is close to and to those she barely knows but who might need a kind thought! One of her sons lives nearby; the other is far away and often in troubled places. So she also "talks" to them while she drives, to feel more connected. My quiet car time is excellent mental creative time for me. I will think about problems and come up with solutions. If it is a new workshop technique or a writing dilemma, I can usually puzzle it out in the car. Doug gave me a small Dictaphone for my birthday, and I use it all the time. When I get one of my ideas while driving, I dare not wait until I get home to write it down; it will be gone by the time I am just a few miles down the road! But I can safely switch on the little recorder and share my ideas before they're lost.

Saving the end of the day for yourself, your family, and thoughtful reflection offsets many of the stresses of everyday life. Pausing to accept inspiration, to give thanks, or to listen to loved ones is one of the greatest gifts you can give yourself. As Ralph Waldo Emerson wrote, "Finish each day and be done with it. You have done what you could. Some blunders and absurdities no doubt crept in; forget them as soon as you can. Tomorrow is a new day; begin it well and serenely and with too high a spirit to be encumbered with your old nonsense." Indeed.

Metal-Gear Candlesticks

Rusted remnants from days gone by can grace your dining-room table or bathroom vanity.

Materials:

- Rusted gears and round hunks of metal, enough to stack in groups of 2 or 3 per candlestick
- Clear, waterproof, UV-resistant glue
- Felt with adhesive backing (one 8- by 10-inch sheet should cover 4 or 5 candlesticks)
- 2- to 3-inch-high pillar candles

1. Clean your gears and metal pieces thoroughly with a powdered cleanser. I find that a sponge with a scrubber side and an old toothbrush do the trick.
2. Let the gears dry completely.
3. Begin stacking the pieces to see what looks good together and what appears to be stable. Remember that you want the stacks to be of varying heights for visual interest.
4. Glue the pieces together with adhesive. Let them dry

Setting a table Salvage Studio style is always a good strategy as an icebreaker. Get the dinner conversations rolling with Metal-Gear Candlesticks.

for a few days before you use them. The candlesticks will be heavy, and you want to make sure you have good adhesion.

5. Cut adhesive-backed felt to cover the bottom of each candlestick, if you are worried about scratches or rust.

6. Place pillar candles on your new candlesticks and enjoy.

Table-Lamp Fountain

The sound of water in the garden can be very soothing, and this water feature is sure to capture anyone's imagination. Choose a lamp that has some character to its stem, with interesting features for the water to run down or splash over. Select a basin to match your garden style: a large wok for an Asian feel or a galvanized bucket for a classic cottage garden, for example.

Materials:

- Table lamp
- Bowl or tub to hold water, suitable in size for the lamp
- Water pump with the capacity to lift water 2 to 3 feet
- Flexible plastic tubing in various diameters, each piece about 2 feet long (see instructions)
- Scrap wood or rocks of equal size, if needed

Tools:

- Wire cutters
- Heavy-duty scissors

1. Remove the socket and all wiring from the lamp. Remove the switch as well, if there is one.

2. Select an appropriate-size vessel for the lamp to sit in and to contain the water. A wok may be big enough for a table lamp. If you already have a water feature that needs a fountain, no other container is needed.

3. Obtain a pump that can lift water to the top of the lamp. Pumps can be found at stores that sell supplies for outdoor water features but can also be found at garden centers, hardware stores, and craft supply houses.

4. Select your tubing. We use clear plastic tubing from a big-box hardware store near our home. This type of tubing works well because it comes in sizes that will nest one into another, one size fitting snugly into the next size larger, making it very easy to adapt different pipe or tubing sizes together. The pipe that

Water fountains can be a welcoming sound for you and your guests. This Table-Lamp Fountain has clear half-marbles in the basin for added sparkle and light.

is used inside of lamps to hold them together and that the electrical wire runs through is one standard size. Tubing with a ⅜-inch outside diameter fits over it nicely and doesn't need a fancy adapter.

5. Push some tubing over the bottom end of the pipe that held the electrical wire. Run the tubing under the lamp base. A table lamp may have a hole where the power switch was; if so, you can run the tubing through it instead of under the base.

6. Connect the tubing to your pump, using short pieces of tubing of intermediate sizes if the fitting on your pump is a different diameter. If your lamp didn't have feet, you may need to set the lamp on something, such as three pieces of wood or three rocks of equal size, so the lamp base doesn't rest right on the tubing.

7. Add water, and plug in your pump. Most pumps have a flow adjustment so you can make the fountain splash more or less, as appropriate.

Recycled Blank Journals

Blank journals constructed from found materials provide the perfect canvas for one's thoughts, musings, and doodles. Two versions are given here—journals made from worn-out novels and those with game-board covers.

Reborn Book Journal

Materials:

- Dilapidated hardcover book, 5½ by 8½ inches or 6 by 9 inches
- 8- by 12-inch sheet of galvanized metal, no more than 0.015 inch thick
- 30 inches of durable tape at least 1 inch wide, such as duct tape, HVAC tape, or strapping tape
- 50 sheets of blank 8½- by 11-inch paper
- Sturdy linen thread or carpet thread in your choice of color
- Embellishments for the cover, such as beads, ribbon, yarn, buttons, or trim
- Heavy-duty adhesive, such as E6000

Tools:

- Sharp craft knife, such as an X-Acto knife
- Ruler
- Tin snips (optional)
- Paper cutter
- 4 large binder clips
- Permanent marking pen

These journals use old Reader's Digest *condensed book covers. Plentiful at thrift stores, many have beautiful covers hidden under the dust jacket.*

- Hand-held power drill
- ³⁄₈-inch drill bit
- Safety goggles
- Yarn or tapestry needle

1. Begin with a tattered book. Don't worry if the cover is falling off; it gives you a head start on deconstruction. If not, use a utility knife to cut along the inside edge between the cover and the book binding, releasing the cover. The inside pages are now perfect material for any decoupage project you desire.

2. Lay the front and back cover on a tabletop. Measure the length of your cover and cut two pieces from the sheet of galvanized metal equal to this length and at least 1 inch in width. You may choose a larger width, depending on the design and shape you desire for your completed journal. Use tin snips or a paper cutter to do the cutting.

3. Place one of the metal strips next to the inside edge of the front book cover. You will use this metal strip to bind your book together. Center the tape so that half of the tape covers the metal strip and half covers the book front. Leave a ¼-inch gap between the metal strip and the book cover when you are taping. This will be the "hinge" that allows your book to open and close. Wrap the tape around the book cover, on both sides. Repeat this process with the back cover, attaching it to the second piece of metal.

4. Measure the dimensions of your completed journal cover, and cut the paper to this measurement, less ½ inch in length and ¼ inch in width, using a paper cutter. (You want the resulting pages to be ¼ inch smaller than the cover on every side but the bind-

ing.) Feel free to include other types of paper that will add a little kick to your writing—a piece of map from a foreign country, a dictionary page with a favorite word, or a newspaper article of special importance are all possible candidates.

5. Now make a sandwich of your book—front cover, journal pages, and back cover. The paper should be flush with the edges of the metal strips and centered between the top and bottom edges. Use binder clips to hold it together.

6. With a ruler, mark a straight line of holes at least ³⁄₈ inch in from the edge of the metal strip, using a permanent marker. You will drill holes through the journal to enable you to hand-sew it together. The number of holes is up to you, but four to seven holes seem to work best for this size journal. Wear safety goggles when drilling.

7. Thread a yarn or tapestry needle with an amount of thread equal to 8 times the length of your journal.

8. Start sewing from the back of the journal, in the second-from-the-top hole, leaving a long tail. Make sure to pull the thread tight as you go through each hole.

9. Bring the thread around the spine to the back of the journal and go back up through the starting hole, then down through the next hole down. Pull the thread tight.

10. Go around the spine again, then down through the hole to the back, up through the next hole down, and around the back again.

11. Keep going like this until you reach the bottom. Go around the bottom of the spine and through the bottom hole again. Now work your way back up, going down through one hole, around the spine, back up

through the next hole, and so on, working your way up. Remember to keep the thread tight.

12. When you reach the top of the journal, go around the top of the spine and through the top hole.

13. End the stitching by going through the starting hole again.

14. To finish, tie off the thread with a knot so the binding won't come loose. Leave long tails so you can add beads or other embellishments to the thread. Remove the binder clips.

15. Embellish your new journal in whatever way you want.

Game-Board Books

Materials:

- Checkerboard or other game board (we love the graphic look of checkerboards)
- Electrical tape
- Black duct tape at least 1 inch wide
- 50 sheets of blank paper
- Sturdy linen thread or carpet thread
- Permanent marking pen

Tools:

- Sharp craft knife, such as an X-Acto knife
- 4 large binder clips
- Ruler
- Paper cutter
- Permanent marking pen
- Hand-held power drill
- ⅜-inch drill bit
- Yarn or tapestry needle

1. With the utility knife, cut the game board in half and then in half again, so you have four squares. You will need only two to make one book. You could make a second one for a friend.

2. Measure approximately 2 inches in from the edge to be bound on both pieces, and cut with the utility knife.

3. Cover the rough cut edges with electrical tape to make a smooth edge.

4. Now duct-tape the 2-inch pieces back to the piece you cut them from, leaving a ¼-inch gap between the two pieces. This will be the "hinge" that allows your book to open and close. The tape should cover the front and back of the gap. Repeat for the back cover.

5. Measure the dimensions of your completed journal cover, and, with a paper cutter, cut the paper to this measurement, less ½ inch in length and ¼ inch in width. (You want the resulting pages to be ¼ inch smaller than the cover on every side but the binding.)

6. Now make a sandwich of your book—front cover, journal pages, and back cover. The paper should be flush with the edge to be bound and centered between the top and bottom edges. Use binder clips to hold it together.

7. With a ruler, mark a straight line of holes at least ⅜ inch in from the left edge of the book, using a permanent marker. You will drill holes through the journal to enable you to hand-sew it together. The number of holes is up to you, but four to seven holes seem to work best for this size journal.

8. Thread a yarn or tapestry needle with an amount of thread equal to 8 times the length of your journal. Bind the journal according to the directions for the Reborn Book Journal, steps 8 through 15.

resources

In this section, we've listed some of our more trusted resources for various supplies, tools, and inspiration that you can find in most parts of the country or easily via the Internet. You can also visit us at the Salvage Studio:

www.thesalvagestudio.com
thesalvagestudio.blogspot.com
www.fourcornersdesign.net

Jewelry Supplies and Tools

www.firemountaingems.com: metal expansion bracelets, findings, supplies
www.riogrande.com: findings, supplies, tools
www.frenchgeneral.com: vintage beading, crafting supplies, kits, tools
www.burntofferings.com: great jewelry tools
www.sleepingdogstudio.etsy.com: vintage jewelry components

Crafting Supplies

www.michaels.com: magnets, jewelry supplies, glues, wire, self-adhesive cork
www.joann.com: jewelry supplies, glues, wire, ribbon, sewing thread, votive candles and holders, foam and chip brushes, metal café rods and clip-on curtain rings, candle wicks
www.artchix.com: clip art, embellishments, transparencies, rubber stamps
www.freedomcrystal.com: chandelier crystals
www.homebrewheaven.com: unused bottle caps
www.papermart.com: large selection of kraft bags, manila tags, cellophane bags, ribbon

A metal pot cover is converted into a magnet board with an apt message.

www.creationstationinc.com: unique blend of recycling and retail

Tools

www.harborfreight.com: huge assortment of tools, including "Big Earl," aka Deep Throat Metal Hand Punch
www.fiskars.com: premier selection of scissors, paper cutters, and other handy tools
www.dremel.com: high-speed rotary drill, ideal for working with metal

Hardware

www.lowes.com: nuts, bolts, hooks, screws, spacers and fittings, upholstery tacks, galvanized metal flashing, sandpaper, duct tape, Atlas gardening gloves, wood molding, Loctite Power Grab adhesive, grout sealer, Johnson's Paste Wax, safety glasses, blackboard paint, variety of twines, ropes, and chains

Miscellaneous

www.re-sources.org: home of the ReStore—vintage and used lamp globes, hardware, locker baskets, and much more
www.etsy.com: online marketplace for buying and selling all things handmade
https://active.boeing.com/assocproducts/surplus/Index.cfm: our Northwest Boeing Surplus store has closed, but check out the ones in California and the Midwest
www.goodwill.org: wooden frames, furniture, silver-plated dishes and silverware, glassware, linens
www.valuevillage.com: wooden frames, furniture, silver-plated dishes and silverware, glassware, linens

acknowledgments

None of this would have been possible without the support and love of our families and friends.

From Amy: Thanks to Stacey, who is the best sister and a premier picker. More than thanks to Monty, my best supporter and ace proofreader.

From Beth: My heartfelt gratitude to Raoul, my husband of 30-plus years, for believing in me through all my creative endeavors (and there was at least one big clunker along the way). An enormous thank-you to my sons, Morgan, a fine dumpster diver, junk hauler, and chuckle generator, and Carlos, a wonderful emotional supporter no matter what part of the world he is living in, and to my daughter-in-law Casey, a swell Studio helper in our early days and deliverer of treasures found in foreign lands, from French *brocantes* to Argentinean antique fairs.

From Lisa: Special thanks to my husband, Doug, who has been a paragon of patience during the comings and goings of all the stuff through our home. He is my project engineer and my Al (tool belt included!). He is also our official Studio Mister, changing light bulbs and waiting on customers, and he makes a mean birdhouse as well. Thanks to my mom, Beth, for teaching me at an early age to reinvent, reuse, and re-create. Ophelia, my original salvage sister, has trolled the streets with me looking through free piles and always has an eye out for good junk. And thanks to my junk-day partner in crime Nancy Fredlund for sharing countless truckloads of treasures and good times. Also, many thanks to Doug's folks, Kenneth

and Eleeta Hilderbrand, and all the Hilderbrand clan for their generosity of spirit and rusty stuff!

From all three of us: A very special thank-you to Kate Rogers, editor in chief of Skipstone, who discovered us at the very beginning and always knew there was a book inside of us. Thanks for bringing it out. And to the "other Kate," photographer Kate Baldwin, who gave our projects a glorious look and was willing to go both high and low to get the perfect shot, and Karen Schober, the designer whose elegant eye captured our message and transformed it on the page. The following folks at Skipstone also played important roles in making this project successful: Janet Kimball, Rebecca Pepper, Shanna Knowlton, and Doug Canfield.

We are indebted to the writers and editors responsible for stories in the press, which helped immensely in spreading the word about our business and creative efforts. This includes Debra Prinzing, our number-one Fairy Godmother, author of numerous garden books and freelance writer extraordinaire; Colleen McBrinn, for that first cover story in the *Seattle Times*, which brought us to the attention of our book editor; and, for numerous ongoing articles, Nicole Tsong, Judy Averill, Robyne Curry, Marty Wingate, John Engstrom, Debra Smith, Melanie Munk, Shannon O'Leary, Pat Tanumihardja, and Sue Romero.

Our deep appreciation goes to the following people: Gillian Matthews, owner of Ravenna Gardens, whose early support of our efforts brought us public attention

A classic typewriter font never goes out of style.

you are invited to a

PARTY

party details here

and loads of goodies. We appreciate her sharing her business smarts with us. Quiet but strong, Mary Kay Lewis of Seattle Goodwill connected us with our prime audience. Amanda Foley of Duo Public Relations gave us the opportunity to work on a fabulous booklet of project ideas for Value Village/Savers, Inc. Lisa B. Hammond lavished splendid styling on our creations for the Value Village booklet, and many of those photos are included in this book.

We couldn't have done it without the best studio helpers ever. Thanks to Karen Herdeck for her whole-hearted assistance at the studio whenever we have needed her and for sharing her son Steven, who has washed, scrubbed, sanded, and painted his heart out to make items studio-ready. Also to Melody Hooper and Un Sin for braving the Northwest elements in the early days of our outdoor sales with style and a smile. Colleen Chapman, Judy Ray, and Kay Dahl for finding and creating glorious treasures to share with our customers.

Warren Bradbury, our landlord, for his support of our endeavors and for leasing us the perfect spot to showcase our salvage creations and host workshops for our creative customers.

And finally an appreciative thanks and pat on the back to the following Salvage Studio workshop participants and other artists, whose creative efforts appear in this book in the Fork Pendant Necklace, the mosaic table, and the Charm Swap Necklace: Sally Jean Alexander ("L" monogram charm), Lisa Call ("HOME" charm), and Caughtredhanded, an Etsy artist (enameled charm); Stacey Duncan; Shari Acuff, Melinda Catalano, Caroline Chastain, Jeanette Coate, Linda Dahl, Beth Evans-Ramos, Sue Frankl, Linda Freeman, Jeannie Glenn, Pam Gonzalez, Yvonne Haines, Debra Harris-Branham, Karen Herdeck, Lisa Hilderbrand, Deb Jensen, Christie Jones, Judy Kullman, Jenifer Matson, Mary Ellen McLelland, Lisa Ross, Diane Vague, Kathy Weisner, and Debbie Woodbury.

Vintage glass coasters reflect a festive mood.

index

Tin cans are the ubiquitous Salvage Studio organizing containers.

Lisa Hilderbrand, Beth Evans-Ramos, and Amy Duncan

Beth Evans-Ramos is a garden stylist and proprietor of Garden Graces, a garden decorating service. In addition to working with private clients, she regularly leads workshops at garden clubs, nurseries, and retailers in the Seattle and Portland areas. One of her most popular topics is "Garden Art From Found Objects, Salvage, and Really Good Junk." She belongs to numerous horticultural organizations and enjoys a wonderful group of friends who meet monthly to share art projects with each other. She lives in Mill Creek, Washington, with her husband, Raoul.

Artist **Amy Duncan** has a long history of creative and ecological endeavors, from teaching one-match fire building and other self-reliance skills to spending 18 years in nonprofit management. Her experiences helped hone her resourcefulness and sense of community. She started her greeting card company, Four Corners Design, in order to create artwork from recycled papers and other materials. Amy lives with her partner, Monty, in Everett, Washington, where their early-century farmhouse is a showplace for Salvage Studio style. Many of the photos in this book were taken at their home.

A garden designer and educator, **Lisa Hilderbrand** promotes sustainable gardening practices in all her work. She has been editor of two quarterly publications, *The Perennial Post* for the Northwest Perennial Alliance and *The Puget Daylily* for the Puget Sound Daylily Club. Lisa has been a member of her local garden club for over a decade. As an avid cook, she is also a member of the Root Connection (a local CSA). She lives in Lynnwood, Washington, with her husband, Doug, and a menagerie of pets.

Photographer **Kate Baldwin** specializes in home, food, people, and other lifestyle subjects. Her clients include Starbucks, Canon USA, Fran's Chocolates, Value Village, *Food Arts Magazine, Seattle Homes & Lifestyles Magazine,* and *Seattle Metropolitan Magazine.* Visit www.katebaldwinphotography.com.

Create a custom gift with a theme. For a friend who loves to cook, marry a vintage cookbook and an old kitchen tool. For a green thumb, combine a garden book with a package of seeds or a weathered garden trowel.

Published by Skipstone, an imprint of The Mountaineers Books

Printed in China

First printing 2008

11 10 09 08   5 4 3 2 1

Copy Editor: Rebecca Pepper

Design: Karen Schober

Cover photograph: Kate Baldwin

Additional photographs provided by Amy Duncan/The Salvage Studio: pages 7 *(bottom photo)*, 9, 11, 12, 60, 107, and 129

All photo styling by Amy Duncan/The Salvage Studio, with the exception of pages 2, 4, 13, 18, 25, 42, 50–51, 57, 65, 74, 77–78, 87, 89, 102, 106, 111, 113–114, 123, 137, 140, 151–152, 157–159, 169, 179, 190, and 199.

Several of Kate Baldwin's photographs first appeared in a calendar and related promotions published by Value Village.

Page 2: Jam jars filled with family photos and mementos greet visitors.

Page 4: An antique teacup paired with special tea makes a thoughtful hostess gift.

Page 6: An old typewriter stand and metal scale each take a role in adding that salvage touch.

Page 7 *(top)*: A Fireplace Tool-Holder caddy adds sparkle to a buffet table.

Page 7 *(middle)*: Handmade charms—a Salvage Studio favorite.

Page 7 *(bottom)*: Rusty garden tools find a second life in a garden display.

ISBN 978-1-59485-079-0

Library of Congress Cataloging-in-Publication Data

Duncan, Amy.
  The Salvage Studio : sustainable home comforts to organize, entertain, and inspire / by Amy Duncan,
Beth Evans-Ramos, and Lisa Hilderbrand ; photography by Kate Baldwin.
     p. cm.
  Includes index.
  ISBN 978-1-59485-079-0 (ppb)
  1. Handicraft. 2. Salvage (Waste, etc.) 3. Recycling (Waste, etc.) 4. House furnishings. I. Evans-Ramos, Beth. II. Hilderbrand, Lisa. III. Title.
  TT157.D83 2008
  745.5--dc22

                    2008017411

Skipstone books may be purchased for corporate, educational, or other promotional sales. For special discounts and information, contact our Sales Department at 1-800-553-4453 or mbooks@mountaineersbooks.org.

Skipstone
1001 SW Klickitat Way
Suite 201
Seattle, Washington 98134
206.223.6303
www.skipstonepress.org
www.mountaineersbooks.org

LIVE LIFE. MAKE RIPPLES.